# Pre-GED
# Social Studies
# Skills

### KENNETH TAMARKIN

*Project Editor*
Karin Evans

C O N T E M P O R A R Y
**BOOKS, INC.**
CHICAGO ■ NEW YORK

**Library of Congress Cataloging-in-Publication Data**

Tamarkin, Kenneth.
    Contemporary's pre-GED social studies.

    1. Social sciences—Examinations, questions, etc.
2. General educational development tests—Study guides.
I. Contemporary Books, inc.    II. Title.    III. Title:
Pre-GED social studies.
H62.3.T36    1987    300'.76    87-433
ISBN 0-8092-5026-8 (pbk.)

Published by Contemporary Books, Inc.
180 North Michigan Avenue, Chicago, Illinois 60601
Manufactured in the United States of America
International Standard Book Number: 0-8092-5026-8

Published simultaneously in Canada by
Fitzhenry & Whiteside
91 Granton Drive
Richmond Hill, Ontario L4B 2N5
Canada

---

*Editorial Director*
Caren Van Slyke

*Editorial*
Mark Boone
Sarah Schmidt
Christine M. Benton

*Production Editor*
Craig Bolt

*Illustrator*
Rosemary Morrissey-Herzberg

*Art & Production*
Princess Louise El
Lois Koehler
Marilyn Vevang

*Cover Design*
Georgene Sainati

*Typography*
Lisa A. Waitrovich

Cover photo © Image Bank

# CONTENTS

# ACKNOWLEDGMENTS

Cartoon on page 3 by Steve Kelley. Reprinted by permission of Copley News Service.

Table on page 6 copyright © 1986 by The New York Times Company. Reprinted by permission.

Excerpt on page 18 from *A People's History of the United States* by Howard Zinn. Copyright © 1980 by Howard Zinn. Reprinted by permission of Harper & Row, Publishers, Inc.

Excerpt on page 27 from *The Black Americans: A History in Their Own Words*, edited by Milton Meltzer. Copyright 1984 by Milton Meltzer. Reprinted by permission of Harper & Row, Publishers.

Excerpt on page 28 from *The Black Americans: A History in Their Own Words*, edited by Milton Meltzer. Copyright 1984 by Milton Meltzer. Reprinted by permission of Harper & Row, Publishers.

Excerpt on page 28 from *Let Them Speak for Themselves*, edited by Christiane Fischer. Copyright 1977 by Archon Books. Reprinted by permission of The Shoe String Press, Inc.

Excerpt on page 42 from *A People's History of the United States* by Howard Zinn. Copyright © 1980 by Howard Zinn. Reprinted by permission of Harper & Row, Publishers, Inc.

Excerpt on page 44 from *A People's History of the United States* by Howard Zinn. Copyright © 1980 by Howard Zinn. Reprinted by permission of Harper & Row, Publishers, Inc.

Graph on page 55 copyright © 1986 by The New York Times Company. Reprinted by permission.

Graph on page 55 copyright © 1985 by The New York Times Company. Reprinted by permission.

Graph on page 56 copyright © 1986 by The New York Times Company. Reprinted by permission.

Table on page 57 reprinted courtesy of *The Boston Globe.* Copyright 1985 *The Boston Globe.*

Graph on page 58 from "Rising Hospital Costs," published by Continental American Life Insurance. Copyright 1986 Continental American Life Insurance. Reprinted by permission.

Graph on page 67 reprinted courtesy of *The Boston Globe.* Copyright 1986 *The Boston Globe.*

Graph on page 79 copyright © 1985 by The New York Times Company. Reprinted by permission.

Map on page 97 from *American History Atlas* by Martin Gilbert. Copyright 1968 by Martin Gilbert. Reprinted by permission of Marboro Books.

Cartoon on page 122 by Gary Trudeau. Copyright 1985, G.B. Trudeau. Reprinted with permission of Universal Press Syndicate. All rights reserved.

Illustration on page 123 from *The Ungentlemanly Art: A History of American Political Cartoons* by Stephen Hess and Milton Kaplan.

Cartoon on page 124 by Oliphant. Copyright 1967, Universal Press Syndicate. Reprinted with permission. All rights reserved.

Illustration on page 125 from *The Ungentlemanly Art: A History of American Political Cartoon* by Stephen Hess and Milton Kaplan.

Cartoon on page 126 by Dick Locher. Reprinted by permission: Tribune Media Services.

Excerpt on page 137 from *The American Reader* by Paul Angle. Copyright 1958. Reprinted by permission of Rand McNally & Company.

Graph on page 138 from *The Facts About Welfare: Being Poor in Massachusetts.* Copyright 1985 by the Office of Research, Planning, and Evaluation, Commonwealth of Massachusetts.

Cartoon on page 139 by Tony Auth. Copyright 1985, *Philadelphia Inquirer.* Reprinted with permission of Universal Press Syndicate. All rights reserved.

# TO THE INSTRUCTOR

This *PRE-GED SOCIAL STUDIES* text is designed to help adult learners develop the critical reading and thinking skills they need to progress to a GED-level textbook. Students working in this book receive a thorough grounding in the organization and comprehension of written material and illustrations. Then they are introduced to the higher-order thinking skills required by the GED Test—analysis, evaluation, and application.

The book emphasizes the step-by-step acquisition of skills rather than discrete knowledge. Materials from the five GED content areas—history, economics, political science, behavioral science, and geography—are represented throughout the text.

Some special features to note are the pretest and posttest, the chapter reviews, and the answer key.

**Pretest** and **Posttest**. These tests are in multiple-choice format, similar to that of the GED Test. Questions are drawn from the entire range of skills and content in the book. Evaluation charts correlated to the chapters help you identify strong and weak areas for each student.

**Chapter Reviews**. These tests, also in multiple-choice format, are brief reviews of the skills taught in the chapter. They focus especially on those skills most needed for the GED Test. Evaluation charts help you see what parts of a chapter a student might need to review before moving on.

**Answer Keys**. A full answer key is located in the back of the text. Students should be encouraged to check their answers as soon as they complete an exercise to ensure that they have mastered the material.

Some exercises in this book ask students to write short answers in their own words. They should make every effort to complete these written exercises. Writing experience will be invaluable to them in preparing for the GED Writing Skills Test, and writing has been shown time after time to be the most effective demonstration of learning and comprehension. When coaching your students in writing tasks, focus on their ideas and how they can be expressed clearly rather than on spelling, grammar, or handwriting.

Finally, encourage your students to read and help them find appropriate materials. The short passages in this book are no substitute for the real reading opportunities available to your students. By becoming more comfortable with reading, they will prepare themselves not only for the GED Tests but for lifelong learning.

# TO THE STUDENT

Welcome to the *PRE-GED SOCIAL STUDIES* book. In this book, you'll be learning the skills you will need when you move on to a GED-level social studies text. You'll learn how to study reading passages as well as illustrations such as charts, graphs, maps, and cartoons.

Before you begin work in this text, take the pretest. It will help you identify chapters to focus on as you move through the text. When you are finished with the text, the posttest will help you evaluate the work you have done.

You'll find answers to all the exercises at the back of the book. Be sure to check yourself at the end of each exercise before you move on. And when an exercise asks you to write, answer fully in your own words. Writing is a very important part of learning. Don't worry about your handwriting or about grammar and spelling. Getting your ideas on paper is what counts.

Finally, read beyond the pages of this book. Read newspapers, magazines, road maps, and anything else you can get your hands on. Reading will help you prepare not only for the GED Tests but also for the rest of your life.

# Pretest

This pretest is a guide to using this book. You should take it before you start working on any of the chapters. The questions will test the social studies reading and reasoning skills covered in this book.

*Directions:* Study each passage or illustration, then answer the questions that follow.

Questions 1–3 are based on the following passage.

There are no beggars in the streets of the Southeast Asian country of Brunei. It is the world's richest state next to the United Arab Emirates. Brunei is ruled by a king, Sultan Hassanal Bolkiah. The sultan keeps a firm hand on his some 200,000 subjects. As the world's richest man, according to *The Guinness Book of Records*, he can afford to take good care of the people of Brunei. In fact, his people don't have to pay any taxes.

Brunei makes about $7 billion every year from the sale of oil and natural gas. After keeping a generous amount of that money for himself, the sultan spends the rest on his people in order to keep them satisfied.

For example, a woman street sweeper earns a tax-free monthly salary of about $1,000. Like all Brunei citizens, the street-sweeping woman receives free medical care. And should her children be good students, they can receive scholarships, grants, and interest-free loans to study at foreign universities. She need not spend a penny for her children's education.

**1.** A sultan is

   **(1)** a king
   **(2)** a rich man
   **(3)** a street sweeper
   **(4)** an Arab
   **(5)** a beggar

**2.** What is the form of government of Brunei?

   **(1)** democracy, rule by the people with free elections
   **(2)** military dictatorship, rule by the head of the armed forces
   **(3)** monarchy, rule by a single member of a royal family
   **(4)** theocracy, rule by priests
   **(5)** oligarchy, rule by a small elite group

**3.** What is the main idea of this passage?

   **(1)** The people of Brunei are involved in decision making and planning for the future of the country.
   **(2)** There are no beggars in the streets of the Southeast Asian country of Brunei.
   **(3)** The wealthy sultan of Brunei keeps control over his people but provides for them generously.
   **(4)** The sultan of Brunei is planning to take over neighboring nations in order to expand his country.
   **(5)** Street sweepers in Brunei earn about $1,000 per month and receive free medical care.

Question 4 is based on the following passage.

> Being a word-processing teacher, I am often called by companies interested in hiring my students. When they ask for a recommendation, they do not first ask about skills, intelligence, age, or appearance. The first question is almost always about attendance and punctuality.

**4.** What do companies value most in their word-processing employees?

   **(1)** potential
   **(2)** attractiveness
   **(3)** youth
   **(4)** dependability
   **(5)** knowledge

Questions 5–7 are based on the following cartoon.

Steve Kelley
San Diego Union
Copley News Service

**Background clues:** In Beirut, Lebanon, members of different factions frequently place bombs in cars. These car bombs are then exploded in public places, creating much damage and terrible injuries and deaths.

**5.** In the cartoon, what are the two people watching?

   **(1)** a modern sculpture exhibit
   **(2)** a traffic jam
   **(3)** an auto junkyard
   **(4)** a demolition derby
   **(5)** cars exploding

**6.** Why do people *usually* hate rush hour?

   **(1)** because it is very dangerous
   **(2)** because they get caught in traffic jams
   **(3)** because they hate to rush
   **(4)** because cars blow up during rush hour
   **(5)** because cars break down during rush hour

**7.** The point of this cartoon is that

   **(1)** car bombs have made Beirut dangerous
   **(2)** cars aren't made like they used to be
   **(3)** new roads must be built in Beirut
   **(4)** Beirut has terrible rush hour traffic
   **(5)** drivers are very reckless in Beirut

Questions 8–10 are based on the following passage.

Caroline rushed out to use her brand-new credit card at Sears. She went straight to the Today's Woman department and picked out three beautiful new dresses. She took the dresses to the cashier and handed over her credit card. The cashier made out a sales slip from Caroline's card. After signing the sales slip, Caroline sailed out of the store with her new dresses.

At the end of the month, Caroline was shocked when she received her statement. She had not realized that the dresses cost so much. The statement listed all her credit purchases and the total amount she owed Sears. She could afford to pay only the minimum payment, not the whole amount she owed. As a result, she had to pay interest to Sears on the unpaid portion.

8. Before she could leave the store with her purchases, Caroline had to

   **(1)** sign the sales slip
   **(2)** pay the total amount due with a check
   **(3)** receive her monthly statement
   **(4)** give her credit card to the cashier
   **(5)** leave a security deposit

9. In which of the following situations would you use a credit card in the same way as Caroline did?

   **(1)** buying dinner for your family at McDonald's
   **(2)** renting an apartment from a realtor
   **(3)** buying new shoes at a shoe store
   **(4)** placing a mail order by phone
   **(5)** withdrawing money from an automatic teller machine

10. Caroline had to pay interest to Sears because

   **(1)** she could not afford to make the minimum payment
   **(2)** whenever you buy something with a credit card, you have to pay interest
   **(3)** she could not afford to pay the full amount she owed
   **(4)** she was so shocked when she received her statement
   **(5)** the dresses she bought were on sale

Questions 11–12 are based on the following graph.

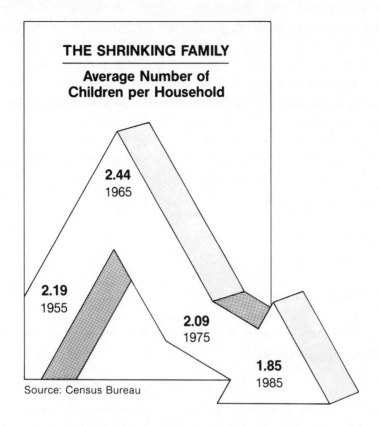

**THE SHRINKING FAMILY**

**Average Number of Children per Household**

2.44
1965

2.19
1955

2.09
1975

1.85
1985

Source: Census Bureau

11. In what year did Americans have the greatest number of children per household?

   (1) 1955
   (2) 1965
   (3) 1975
   (4) 1980
   (5) 1985

12. Which of the following is a reasonable conclusion based on this graph?

   (1) American children generally have fewer brothers and sisters than was the case twenty years ago.
   (2) Americans are earning more money than they did thirty years ago.
   (3) There will not be enough elementary schools in five years unless more are built.
   (4) Most Americans are deciding not to have any children.
   (5) There has been an increase in single-parent households.

The United States can be thought of as a land of invention. For example, in the area of transportation, America has been responsible for more progress than any other nation in the world. American firsts include the steamboat, the airplane, and the nuclear submarine. The nineteenth century's most extensive railroad system was built in our country. In addition, the mass production of automobiles began in the United States, and our highway system is the best in the world.

**13.** In the area of transportation, the United States has

   **(1)** been a world leader
   **(2)** concentrated on the automobile
   **(3)** neglected the railroads
   **(4)** followed progress in Europe
   **(5)** resisted change

Questions 14–15 are based on the following chart.

## Strategic imports

(Averages, in percent, 1981-84)

| | Industrial diamond stones | Platinum group metals | Chromium | Vanadium | Manganese | Uranium | Gold |
|---|---|---|---|---|---|---|---|
| Share of U.S. imports originating in South Africa | 67 | 67 | 56 | 38 | 33 | 24 | n.a. |
| South Africa's share of world reserves | 7 | 81 | 84 | 47 | 71 | 14 | 55.1 |
| South Africa's share of world production | 14.8 | 43.2 | n.a. | 42.2 | 14.7 | 14.8 | 47.0 |

Sources: U.S. Department of Commerce; U.S. Bureau of Mines; Organization for Economic Cooperation and Development

**14.** What percentage of the platinum group metals imported to the United States came from South Africa?

   **(1)** 14%
   **(2)** 43.2%
   **(3)** 56%
   **(4)** 67%
   **(5)** 81%

**15.** Industrial diamonds, platinum group metals, chromium, vanadium, manganese, and uranium are all important to American industry. What does the chart tell you about the relationship of South Africa to the United States?

**(1)** The United States has no relationship with South Africa.
**(2)** South Africa relies on the United States for valuable metals.
**(3)** The United States could get along easily without imports from South Africa.
**(4)** South Africa provides the United States with important raw materials.
**(5)** South Africa lacks natural mineral resources.

Questions 16–18 are based on the following passage.

In May 1607, the first permanent English colony in what is now the United States was founded at Jamestown, Virginia. The colonists built their village on a terrible swamp, and then the men spent their time looking for gold. The entire colony would have starved if not for the help of the native chief Powhatan, who gave the settlers food.

The colony struggled along until John Rolfe discovered the American tobacco plant. Virginia began to export tobacco to Europe, where it became very popular. The success of the Virginia colony was assured.

**16.** After building their village, the first settlers

**(1)** planted tobacco
**(2)** attacked the Indians
**(3)** searched for gold
**(4)** planted food crops
**(5)** befriended and helped the Indians

**17.** The colonists needed help from the Indians

**(1)** because they did not know how to grow tobacco in Virginia
**(2)** because they did not produce enough food
**(3)** to prevent slavery in Virginia
**(4)** to build the village of Jamestown
**(5)** to export tobacco to Europe

**18.** There is enough information in the passage to determine that

  **(1)** in order to survive, the settlers had to defeat the Indians
  **(2)** the desire for religious freedom was the reason that the settlers came to Virginia
  **(3)** the settlers needed help from the Indians in order to grow tobacco
  **(4)** the settlers believed in democracy and equality for all people
  **(5)** the growing and exporting of tobacco led to the success of the Virginia colony

Questions 19–20 are based on the following map.

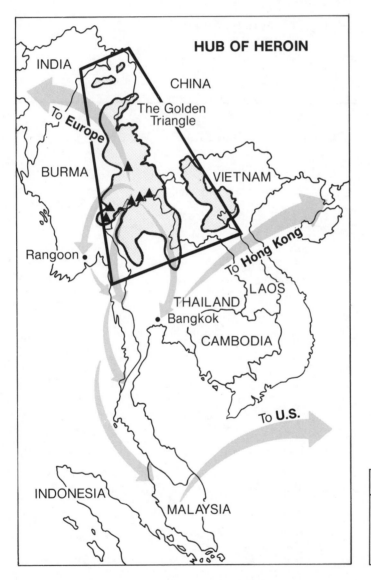

**HUB OF HEROIN**

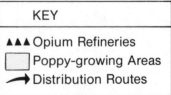

KEY

▲▲▲ Opium Refineries
☐ Poppy-growing Areas
➤ Distribution Routes

**19.** The opium refineries in the Golden Triangle are all in

**(1)** Bangkok
**(2)** Europe
**(3)** Rangoon
**(4)** India
**(5)** poppy-growing areas

**20.** From Malaysia, heroin is sent to

**(1)** Thailand
**(2)** Burma
**(3)** Hong Kong
**(4)** the U.S.
**(5)** Europe

Questions 21–22 are based on the following passage.

The plow played a vital role for men in search of the American promise of opportunity and independence. The wilderness was the frontier for American men. As long as they could clear new land, plow it, and grow something on it, it was their land. The plow set them free.

However, the city was the frontier for American women. The typewriter gave them a way to earn money and the opportunity to set a course of their own. The business office, not the wilderness, would give women the chance to control their own lives.

**21.** According to the passage, the machine that most helped women gain economic independence was

**(1)** the sewing machine
**(2)** the typewriter
**(3)** the plow
**(4)** the electric mixer
**(5)** the automobile

**22.** The passage describes different opportunities for American women and American men. The key difference the writer describes is that

**(1)** women were more dependent than men
**(2)** women preferred to live in cities while men preferred to live in log cabins
**(3)** women preferred staying at home while men preferred change and adventure
**(4)** cities offered women the independence and opportunity that men found in the wilderness
**(5)** women planned for the future while men lived for the present

Questions 23–24 are based on the following passage.

In the 1840s, many Americans believed in "manifest destiny," the idea that the United States had the right to control all the land from the Atlantic to the Pacific. President Polk used the theory of manifest destiny to justify declaring war on Mexico. As a result of this war, Mexico lost half of her territory and the United States gained most of its southwestern lands, including California.

**23.** Which of the following statements is an opinion?

**(1)** Mexico lost half of her territory after losing the Mexican War.
**(2)** The United States took over California as a result of the Mexican War.
**(3)** The term *manifest destiny* was coined by John L. O'Sullivan.
**(4)** Polk was president of the United States during the Mexican War.
**(5)** The United States had the right to take over the entire continent.

**24.** The main idea of this paragraph is that

**(1)** the United States used "manifest destiny" to justify taking over half of Mexico
**(2)** Mexico lost half her territory in the Mexican War
**(3)** the American form of government needs an entire continent to function well
**(4)** the United States was right to conquer half of Mexico in order to spread democracy
**(5)** Mexico provoked the United States into war

**25.** This ad wants you to believe that Gisell perfume

**(1)** is used by many famous people
**(2)** will make a woman feel special
**(3)** is a good buy
**(4)** is used by more women than any other perfume
**(5)** will drive men wild

Questions 26–28 are based on the following passage.

As in many other southern towns, many people in Eastman, Georgia, used to work in a textile mill. After eighty years of operation, the Reeves Brothers mill closed, laying off 340 people. The economy of this little town was hurt badly by the loss of jobs and wages from the mill.

Bit by bit, however, the town is rebounding from the mill closing. The Standard Candy Company had only sixty part-time employees a year ago. Now Standard Candy has 150 full-time workers and expects to have 300 by three years from now. Another company, Reynolds Aluminum, is adding fifty employees to its payroll. A local welding company is expanding, and so is another new, small candy company. In addition, a large discount store will be opening its doors in another year, providing even more jobs.

Perhaps the best news for the future of Eastman is a new Georgia highway that will run right through it. The highway will be finished in three years and will connect Georgia's largest city, Atlanta, with the Georgia seacoast. Because of the highway, products made in Eastman will be easier to ship to other places. The highway will also allow Eastman to attract tourists driving from Atlanta to the beaches.

**26.** The new highway running through Eastman will

(1) run from Atlanta to New York City
(2) allow residents to commute easily to work in the textile mill
(3) attract tourists driving to Florida
(4) make Eastman less attractive to new businesses
(5) connect Atlanta to the Georgia coast

**27.** Over the next five years, it is likely that

(1) the 340 jobs Eastman lost when the mill closed will be replaced by other jobs
(2) the population of Eastman will decline rapidly
(3) many residents of Eastman will turn to farming to make their living
(4) most people who were laid off when the mill closed will still be out of work
(5) a major state highway running through Eastman will close

**28.** Which of the following strategies could best help another small Southern town rebound from a mill closing?

   **(1)** Residents should relocate to areas where mills are still open.
   **(2)** The town should work to attract new businesses to the area.
   **(3)** Mill workers who are laid off by the closing should collect unemployment.
   **(4)** The town should improve schools and recreational programs for children.
   **(5)** The town should build a new highway.

Questions 29–30 are based on the following passage.

New research shows that friendship is very important in the lives of elderly people. A study of senior citizens showed that these older people want to give to and do things for their friends. Researcher Karen Roberto thinks that older people feel more independent and more able when they can give to others.

Roberto also reports that elderly men and elderly women have different kinds of friendships. The men tended to do things with their friends—go places or play games. The women, on the other hand, were more emotionally involved with their friends.

**29.** According to Roberto, what is a possible reason why elderly people want to give to and do things for their friends?

   **(1)** Many older people don't often see their families, so they want to do things for their friends.
   **(2)** They don't have enough to do to keep busy, and doing things for others helps pass the time.
   **(3)** They feel that their friends are in need of assistance.
   **(4)** Doing things for others makes them feel more independent.
   **(5)** There aren't enough volunteer opportunities for older people.

**30.** Based on the information in the passage, which of the following statements is true?

   **(1)** Older men are happier with their friendships than older women.
   **(2)** Elderly people don't have enough friends.
   **(3)** Older men are less emotionally involved with their friends than older women are.
   **(4)** Older people need friends because their families don't care for them.
   **(5)** Senior citizen housing encourages older people to form healthy and lasting friendships.

# PRETEST EVALUATION CHART

Check your answers on pages 14–15; then come back to this chart and find the number of each question you missed and circle it in the second column. Then decide which chapters you should concentrate on.

| | Skill | Item Numbers | Number Correct |
|---|---|---|---|
| **Ch. 1** | Finding details | 21, 26 | _____ /7 |
| | Words in context | 1 | |
| | Restating information | 2 | |
| | Summarizing information | 13 | |
| | Main idea of a paragraph | 24 | |
| | Main idea of a passage | 3 | |
| **Ch. 2** | Locating information on a chart | 14 | _____ /4 |
| | Locating information on a graph | 11 | |
| | Locating information on a map | 20 | |
| | Using a map key | 19 | |
| **Ch. 3** | Sequence | 8, 16 | _____ /4 |
| | Cause and effect | 10 | |
| | Compare and contrast | 22 | |
| **Ch. 4** | Fact and opinion | 23 | _____ /7 |
| | Inference | 17 | |
| | Political cartoons | 5, 6, 7 | |
| | Hypothesis | 29 | |
| | Predicting outcomes | 27 | |
| **Ch. 5** | Adequacy of information | 18, 30 | _____ /6 |
| | Intepreting charts | 15 | |
| | Interpreting graphs | 12 | |
| | Values | 4 | |
| | Propaganda | 25 | |
| **Ch. 6** | Application | 9, 28 | _____ /2 |

## PRETEST ANSWER KEY

**1.** (1) The passage says that Sultan Hassanal Bolkiah is a king.

**2.** (3) The passage tells you that Brunei is ruled by a king. You can eliminate the other answers.

**3.** (3) This choice combines all the ideas in the passage: the ruler of Brunei is very rich, he rules firmly, and he spends a lot of his money on his people.

**4.** (4) The writer tells you that the companies are most concerned with attendance and punctuality. If a worker comes to work every day on time, the worker is dependable.

**5.** (5) All around the two people are exploding cars.

**6.** (2) The answer to this question comes from general knowledge. The contrast between a normal rush hour and rush hour in Beirut is the key to the humor in this cartoon.

**7.** (1) The cartoon implies that car bombs are common in Beirut. The bombs are very dangerous.

**8.** (1) The passage states that, after she signed the sales slip, Caroline left the store.

**9.** (3) A shoe store is the only place among the choices where you could buy something in person with a credit card.

**10.** (3) The passage says that Caroline could not afford to pay the whole amount she owed. As a result, she had to pay interest on the remaining amount.

**11.** (2) The highest point on the graph is labeled 1965.

**12.** (1) In 1965, there was an average of 2.44 children per household. In 1985, that number had dropped to 1.85. With fewer children per household, you could conclude that children had fewer brothers and sisters.

**13.** (1) The passage describes different ways that the United States has been a world leader in transportation.

**14.** (4) Find the column labeled "Platinum group metals." Then find the row labeled "Share of U.S. imports originating in South Africa." The percentage in the box where the row and column cross is 67%.

**15.** (4) These materials are important to U.S. industry. The chart shows you that South Africa sells a lot of these materials to the United States.

**16.** (3) The passage states that the colonists built their village and then spent their time looking for gold.

**17.** (2) The passage tells you that the entire colony would have starved if Powhatan had not given the settlers food. A likely explanation for this situation is that the settlers were not producing enough food.

**18.** (5) The passage states that the colony limped along until Rolfe discovered tobacco and that Virginia began exporting tobacco to Europe. The writer concludes by saying that the success of the Virginia colony was assured, implying that tobacco was the reason for that success.

**19.** (5) Opium refineries are marked on the map by triangles. All the triangles are in the gray poppy-growing areas.

**20.** (4) Distribution routes are marked on the map by arrows. The arrow from Malaysia, in the bottom center of the map, is labeled "to U.S."

**21.** (2) The passage says that the typewriter gave women a way to earn money.

**22.** (4) The first paragraph says that men found independence in the wilderness. The second paragraph describes the city as the place where women found the opportunity for independence.

**23.** (5) This idea was believed by many Americans, but it was their opinion, not a fact. All the other choices are facts.

**24.** (1) This choice pulls together all the ideas in the paragraph.

**25.** (2) The ad tells you that giving a woman the perfume says to her, "You're special."

**26.** (5) The passage says that the highway will connect Atlanta with the Georgia seacoast.

**27.** (1) The passage describes ways in which new jobs are coming into Eastman because of new and expanding businesses. It also predicts that the highway, to be completed in three years, will help Eastman's manufacturing and tourist businesses.

**28.** (2) New businesses are helping to bring new jobs to Eastman. Other small towns that have lost jobs through mill closings would also benefit if new businesses moved in.

**29.** (4) The passage tells you that Roberto thinks that older people feel more independent when they can give to others.

**30.** (3) The passage tells you that men tended to do things with their friends while women were more emotionally involved with their friends.

# 1 Understanding What You Read

In order to understand social studies fully, you will need to master the skills in this book. One of the most basic reading skills is finding details and facts. Another basic reading skill is understanding the meaning of unfamiliar words. In this chapter, you'll start by working on these two skills.

Later in the chapter, you'll work on putting ideas in other words by summarizing and restating. Then you'll practice finding the main idea. Studying these skills will lay the groundwork for reading and understanding social studies.

# LOCATING DETAILS AND FACTS

## Question Words

The first step in understanding what you read is picking out *details*. You look for facts to answer six basic questions: Who? What? Where? When? How? and Why? In the following example, Judge Phillips needs to use all six questions in order to understand the case.

**JUDGE:** *Whom* are you here to represent?

**LAWYER:** My client is Elisa Canter.

**JUDGE:** *Why* is she here?

**LAWYER:**   To file for divorce.

**JUDGE:**   *What* are the grounds for divorce?

**LAWYER:**   Cruel and abusive treatment.

**JUDGE:**   *When* did this alleged treatment take place?

**LAWYER:**   Last Friday night.

**JUDGE:**   *Where* did it happen?

**LAWYER:**   At their home.

**JUDGE:**   *How* did her husband abuse her?

**LAWYER:**   He beat her up.

In order for the judge to make a decision, she must ask *who, what, when, where, how,* and *why.* To understand the details of what you read, you should be able to find the answers to these questions.

# Finding the Information

Now practice finding information for questions asking *who, what, when, where, how,* and *why.* Read the following paragraph. See if you can match the correct answer with each question. Write the letter of the answer in the space provided.

Yip Harburg, the songwriter, told Studs Terkel about the year 1932: "I was walking along the street at that time, and you'd see the bread lines. The biggest one in New York City was owned by William Randolph Hearst. He had a big truck with several people on it, and big cauldrons of hot soup, bread. Fellows with burlap on their feet were lined up all around Columbus Circle, and went for blocks and blocks around the park, waiting."

_____ **1.** Where was this bread line?

_____ **2.** Who was waiting in the bread line?

_____ **3.** When did this scene take place?

_____ **4.** What was being served at the bread line?

_____ **5.** How did William Randolph Hearst give out food to poor people?

(a) He had a big truck with several people on it.

(b) in 1932

(c) in New York City

(d) fellows with burlap on their feet

(e) hot soup and bread

Make sure you tried each question in the example above on your own before you read the following explanations. Did you match one answer to each question?

**1.** (c) To answer this *where* question, you must find the name of the place. The place is given in the second sentence: New York City.

**2.** (d) To answer this *who* question, you must find the name or a description of people in the bread line. They are described in the last sentence: "Fellows with burlap on their feet were lined up. . . ."

**3.** (b) To answer this *when* question, you must find the date. In the first sentence, 1932 is given as the year the events of the passage took place.

**4.** (e) To answer this *what* question, you must look for the name or description of the thing served. In the third sentence, you read that hot soup and bread were served on the truck.

**5.** (a) To answer this *how* question, you must find the way Hearst gave out the food. The third sentence states, "He had a big truck with several people on it. . . ."

## EXERCISE 1: FINDING DETAILS

*Directions:* Following each paragraph are detail questions. Write your answer to each question in the space provided.

> In 1960, television helped elect a new president. Young John Kennedy defeated Richard Nixon in their famous television debate. Many political writers believe that Kennedy's good performance on television led to his narrow victory in the election.

**1.** Who were involved in the important televised debates of 1960?

_____

**2.** According to many political writers, how did Kennedy win the 1960 presidential election?

_____

In 1968, the Public Service Company of New Hampshire began building a nuclear power plant in Seabrook, New Hampshire. There are many problems with the Seabrook Nuclear Power Plant. If there is ever an accident at the plant, all 100,000 people vacationing on nearby beaches would have to leave on one two-lane highway. The project has money problems as well. But the biggest problem for the builders of the Seabrook plant is a group of people called the Clamshell Alliance. In May 1977, 1,414 members of the Clamshell Alliance were arrested for occupying the plant site. Ten years later they are still actively trying to prevent the completion and opening of the plant.

**3.** Where is the proposed power plant located?

_____

**4.** When were 1,414 Clamshell Alliance members arrested for protesting the Seabrook Power Plant?

_____

**5.** If there were an accident at the plant, how would vacationers have to leave the area?

_____

**6.** What is the Clamshell Alliance trying to do?

_____

## EXERCISE 2: MORE PRACTICE IN FINDING DETAILS

_Directions:_ This exercise is in multiple-choice format. Read the paragraphs. Then answer the questions that follow.

When George L. Belair was running for city council in Minneapolis, Minnesota, he gave away some Twinkies to senior citizens. Under Minnesota law, candidates for office are not allowed to give away food or drinks in order to get votes. Because of this law, Mr. Belair was arrested. He will now have to prove in court that he was not trying to get votes by giving away the cakes.

**1.** To whom did Mr. Belair give the Twinkies?

    **(1)** the court
    **(2)** his opponent
    **(3)** the city council
    **(4)** senior citizens
    **(5)** candidates

**2.** Why was Mr. Belair arrested?

   **(1)** He tried to bribe a police officer by giving him Twinkies.
   **(2)** It's illegal to give away a product that people usually have to pay for.
   **(3)** He had stolen the Twinkies he was giving away.
   **(4)** He gave free drinks to senior citizens.
   **(5)** In Minnesota, candidates cannot give away food to get votes.

   Since 1945, the human race has had to face the possibility of its own destruction. In August of that year, an American airplane dropped the first atomic bomb on Hiroshima, Japan. That single bomb destroyed the entire city. In the years since that first explosion, the United States has built enough bombs to destroy the entire world. The Soviet Union has also built enough bombs to wipe out the human race. Great Britain, France, India, and China also have nuclear weapons. Humanity's future now depends on countries settling their differences peacefully.

**3.** The first atomic bomb was dropped by

   **(1)** the Soviet Union
   **(2)** the United States
   **(3)** Germany
   **(4)** Japan
   **(5)** China

**4.** What was the result when the bomb was dropped on Hiroshima?

   **(1)** The United Nations was formed.
   **(2)** The Soviet Union built many bombs.
   **(3)** The entire city was destroyed.
   **(4)** The United States destroyed the entire world.
   **(5)** An American airplane went down.

   For many years, large companies have fought with their workers' unions. But greater competition from overseas has forced both sides to look again at the way they work together. One example of a new approach occurred at the Chrysler Corporation. The United Auto Workers worked together with the company and the government to save Chrysler. Workers accepted pay cuts while the company got back on its feet. The president of the auto workers' union became a member of the board of directors. During the crisis, workers and management tried to become partners instead of enemies.

5. Why did the union and management of Chrysler decide to work together?

   **(1)** The government forced them to work together.
   **(2)** The union president joined the board of directors.
   **(3)** The company got tired of fighting with the union.
   **(4)** Greater competition from overseas threatened the company.
   **(5)** Workers and management wanted to become partners.

6. Who accepted pay cuts while Chrysler got back on its feet?

   **(1)** large companies
   **(2)** the union president
   **(3)** the board of directors
   **(4)** management
   **(5)** workers

**Answers start on page 198.**

# UNDERSTANDING UNFAMILIAR WORDS

## Using the Context

When reading social studies, you may find unfamiliar words. When you see words you don't know, understanding what you read is harder. Until you figure out the unknown word, what you read might not make sense to you.

You could find out the meaning of a word by looking it up in the dictionary. But sometimes you can't do that—you don't have time, or no dictionary is handy. And even if you do look up a word in the dictionary, sometimes the definition is hard to understand. However, you can often figure out the meaning of a word by reading the words around it. This is called using the *context* (words around a word) to figure out the meaning of an unknown word. In this section, you'll practice looking at the context of unfamiliar words to find their meaning.

## Synonym, Definition, and Comparison Clues

Often in social studies reading, you will find a *synonym*—another word with almost the same meaning—near an unfamiliar word. Or you might find an explanation or definition of what the unknown word means. Sometimes in the passage you will find a comparison with something you know or understand. All of these clues can help you figure out what the unknown word means. Here's an example:

> Calvin Coolidge once said, "When more and more people are thrown out of work, **unemployment** results."

In this example, there is a definition clue. The word *unemployment* is explained directly in the sentence. Underline the definition of unemployment in the quotation above. Unemployment happens when people are thrown out of work.

Now try another example. Underline the comparison in the following passage that is a clue to the meaning of the word *homogeneous*.

> The girls at Whitman High School can only be described as **homogeneous**. Like a school of identically shaped and colored fish, they wear the same clothes, eat the same food, and even talk the same.

▶ What does *homogeneous* mean? _____

Homogeneous means "alike." The comparison clue is "Like a school of identically shaped and colored fish. . . ." In addition, the passage says that the girls dress, eat, and talk alike.

## EXERCISE 3: SYNONYM, DEFINITION, AND COMPARISON CLUES

*Directions:* In the space provided, write the meaning of the word or phrase in **dark type**. Use the context clues in the sentences—look for a synonym, definition, or comparison.

1. The **Bessemer process** of steel making consists of blowing air through molten iron to get rid of impurities.

   Bessemer process _____

2. Like the patent medicine sold by phony doctors to cure all kinds of illnesses, industrial growth was supposed to be a **panacea** for the nation's ills.

   panacea _____

3. President Andrew Jackson began a dubious American political tradition, the widespread use of **patronage**—giving jobs and favors for political reasons.

   patronage _____

4. The Standard Oil Company created a **monopoly** in the oil industry, controlling production and crushing its competition.

   monopoly _____

5. Worker **productivity** has increased as new machines allow one laborer to make much more than before.

   productivity _____

6. When the **transcontinental** railroad was completed in 1869, a person could travel by train from the Atlantic to the Pacific Oceans.

   transcontinental _____

**Answers start on page 198.**

# Antonym and Contrast Clues

In the last section you learned how to figure out the meaning of a word when nearby words had a similar meaning. In this section, you will figure out the meaning of an unknown word when the nearby words have an *opposite* meaning. Read the example sentence below.

> As the strike entered its ninth week, the workers had to decide whether to **persist** or to give up.

▶ What does *persist* mean? _____

This example has an antonym clue. An *antonym* is a word that is the opposite of a given word. In this example, the workers are choosing between two choices: to persist or to give up. You can conclude that the opposite of *to persist* is *to give up*. Therefore, *to persist* means *to keep trying*. Now try another example.

> Despite government claims that people were calming down, the violence continued to **escalate**.

▶ What is the meaning of *escalate*? _____

This example has a contrast clue. A situation is described that is **in contrast to**, or the opposite of, another situation. In this sentence, *escalating violence* is the opposite of people becoming calm. You can conclude that **to escalate** means *to increase*.

Clue words such as *unlike, despite,* and *although* may help you identify antonym and contrast clues, as in the following example:

> **Unlike** children in **wealthy** Kenwood, many children in **impoverished** Garfield Park go hungry.

## EXERCISE 4: ANTONYM AND CONTRAST CLUES

*Directions:* The sentences on the left have antonym or contrast clues. Each sentence contains words or phrases with opposite meanings. Choose the letter of the correct answer to each question on the right.

After years without restrictions on the number of immigrants allowed into the country, Congress passed the first **quota** law in 1921.

**1.** A quota is

   **(a)** a person from another country

   **(b)** a numerical limit

   **(c)** an economic goal

In the late nineteenth century, new cities grew in the Northeast and Midwest. The **squalor** of these new industrial cities contrasted sharply with the beauty of the surrounding countryside.

**2.** Squalor is

   **(a)** filth

   **(b)** large size

   **(c)** beauty

After living in the well-watered East, many pioneers were unprepared for the **arid** West.

**3.** According to the passage, the West was

   **(a)** well-watered

   **(b)** dry

   **(c)** empty

Despite the desire of Indians to live **amicably** with white people, treaties were broken and fighting broke out.

**4.** To live amicably is to

   **(a)** control others

   **(b)** be peaceful

   **(c)** better oneself

Unlike the Native American tribes, which only wanted to keep their own lands, the United States followed an **expansionist** policy in the nineteenth century.

**5.** An expansionist policy favors

   **(a)** improving relations with neighbors

   **(b)** getting rid of foreign influence

   **(c)** making the nation larger

**Answers start on page 198.**

# Using the Sense of the Passage

Sometimes an important word is not defined directly. There may not be any antonyms or contrast clues. In these cases, you must determine the meaning of the word by reading the entire passage. Sometimes you might be able to figure out the meaning of the unknown word by looking at examples given in the rest of the passage. Other times you will have to rely on your overall understanding of the meaning of the passage, as in the following example.

> The great American **megalopolis** stretches over four hundred miles from Boston to Washington, D.C. Including such cities as New York, Philadelphia, Newark, and Baltimore, it is the largest urban area in the world.

▶ What is a megalopolis?

   **(1)** a large city and its suburbs
   **(2)** a state government
   **(3)** a group of connected cities and suburbs
   **(4)** a large lottery

You were right if you chose (3). The phrase *stretches over* gives you the sense of a connected or continuous area. Since the megalopolis includes many cities, it would have to include suburban areas lying between the cities.

## EXERCISE 5: USING THE SENSE OF THE PASSAGE

*Directions:* Answer the questions that follow each passage.

> At **the turn of the century**, American life was changing rapidly. The most visible change was in transportation. Cars were beginning to be seen all over the country. And in 1903 the Wright brothers made the first airplane flight. Motorized vehicles were becoming our primary way of getting around.

**1.** When is meant by *the turn of the century* in this passage?

   **(1)** around 1700
   **(2)** around 1800
   **(3)** around 1900
   **(4)** in 1903

> **Congestion** in a big city can't be avoided. One experiences it everywhere. Traffic jams are a constant irritation, making one's feet the fastest way to travel most of the time. A crowded elevator and tightly packed subway train are other reminders of congestion in the city. One can't even escape from lack of space by dying, since cemeteries are just as densely populated as the cities they serve.

**2.** *Congestion* means

(1) illness
(2) confusion
(3) overcrowding
(4) poverty

> She was a scrawny hardbitten little woman and she greeted me with that politely blank stare which Negroes often reserve for hostile whites or prying members of their own race.
> I had been directed to her tenement in Richmond's **ramshackle** Negro section by another woman, a gray-haired old grandmother whose **gnarled** hands had been stemming tobacco for five decades.

**3.** *Ramshackle* means

(1) run-down
(2) modern
(3) quaint
(4) historic

**4.** *Gnarled* means

(1) pretty
(2) smooth
(3) twisted
(4) black

**Answers start on page 198.**

# RESTATING AND SUMMARIZING

## Restating Details and Facts

> "Mom, you're going to love your new home. There will be people there your own age. There will be a nurse on duty at all times. You'll get the medical care you need."
> "So you've decided to ship your poor old mother to a nursing home."

Mom has just restated the facts in different words. Being able to *restate* details and facts in different words is an important step in understanding what you read. Here's an example of a passage and questions that ask you to identify material that is stated in different words.

(1) One way out pointed north. (2) There were jobs up there, people said. (3) And they let you live a little. (4) The war that had exploded in Europe in 1914 had cut off the flow of immigrants from the old countries. (5) Northern factories, booming on war orders, were short of labor. (6) Manufacturers sent agents south to recruit black workers. (7) They came with free railroad passes in hand or offered cheap tickets to groups of migrants. (8) A "Northern fever" seized the Blacks of the South.

Read the following statements. If the statement is a correct restatement of the sentence or sentences indicated, write *C* in the blank and underline the part of the passage it restates. If not, write *I* for incorrect.

_____ **1.** Northern manufacturers preferred southern black workers to European immigrants. (sentences 4–5)

_____ **2.** Employers gave southern blacks assistance in moving north to work. (sentence 7)

Read the following explanations to see how you could think through this example correctly:

**1.** I    The passage states that the war in Europe had cut off the flow of immigrants and the factories were short of labor. It doesn't say anything about what kind of workers the manufacturers preferred.

**2.** C    This sentence restates the information in sentence 7. The passage says that the agents of manufacturers encouraged blacks to go north to work by giving them free or cheap railroad tickets.

## EXERCISE 6: RECOGNIZING RESTATED INFORMATION

*Directions:* After reading each passage, read the sentences that follow. If you think that the statement is a correct restatement of part of the passage, write *C* for correct. If not, write *I* for incorrect.

(1) We had good schools in French Corral, better than they had in San Francisco at that time. (2) Most of our teachers were young men who were college graduates out from the East for a chance to make money and go back to take up further studies. (3) One of our best teachers was Marion McCarroll Scott, a young Southerner. (4) The various teachers found a congenial atmosphere in our home and spent many evenings playing cards with my parents.

_____ **1.** The young teachers who came to French Corral from the East wanted to start a new life and settle there. (sentence 2)

_____ **2.** Teachers were always welcome in the writer's home. (sentence 4)

(1) For many years, the United States has interfered in the affairs of Nicaragua. (2) In the 1850s, Cornelius Vanderbilt organized a steamboat company to transport freight across Nicaragua. (3) Because Vanderbilt wanted political stability in the region, he financed William Walker to overthrow the existing government. (4) In 1856, Walker became president of Nicaragua. (5) Walker made the mistake of quarreling with Vanderbilt and seizing his ships. (6) This led to an invasion of Nicaragua by a Central American coalition supported by Vanderbilt. (7) This coalition deposed President William Walker.

_____ **3.** Vanderbilt worked for the establishment of democracy in Nicaragua. (sentence 3)

_____ **4.** Walker lost his presidency when he lost Vanderbilt's support. (sentences 6–7)

**Answers start on page 198.**

## EXERCISE 7: RESTATING INFORMATION IN YOUR OWN WORDS

_Directions:_ Read each passage, then answer the questions that follow in your own words.

Rockefeller's company, Standard Oil, managed to put a lot of other oil companies out of business. First Rockefeller pressured railroads into lowering their freight charges for Standard Oil shipments. Then he could charge less for his products than other oil companies because his freight costs were lower. If other oil companies managed to stay in business anyway, Rockefeller had another tactic. He would lower his prices in their area until Standard Oil had lured away all the other companies' customers.

**1.** How did Standard Oil reduce its freight costs?

_____

**2.** How did Standard Oil wipe out its competition?

_____

The most successful of the early labor unions was the American Federation of Labor (AFL), founded in 1886 under the leadership of Samuel Gompers. The AFL was a united group of craft unions. Unlike the unsuccessful labor unions, the AFL did not sponsor its own political candidates. It also did not demand radical social change. Instead, the AFL worked toward concrete goals such as higher wages and shorter work hours.

**3.** What types of goals did the American Federation of Labor work toward?

_____

**4.** What did the unsuccessful early labor unions do?

_____

**Answers start on page 199.**

# Summarizing Details and Facts

When you summarize, you make one statement that gives the main point of a group of details or facts. A summary should contain all of the important ideas. In the following example, practice finding a summary statement that pulls together all the ideas in the original sentences. Read the following three statements:

Henry Ford produced the first low-cost automobile.

Ford was able to save money through mass production of his automobile.

Millions of people were able to own a car for the first time because of the low cost.

Now place a check before the sentence that best summarizes the three statements. Make sure that the one you choose contains <u>all</u> of the important ideas from the three statements.

_____ Mass production has made many products affordable.
_____ By creating the mass-produced car, Henry Ford changed America.
_____ By using mass production, Ford produced a low-cost car that was bought by millions of people.

The last choice is the correct one: By using mass production (second statement), Ford produced a low-cost car (first statement) that was bought by millions of people (third statement). You can see that all the important ideas are covered.

## EXERCISE 8: SUMMARIZING FACTS

*Directions:* Following each group of statements are three possible summary sentences. Circle the letter of the best summary. Make sure all the important ideas are included in the summary you choose.

1. Coleco almost went bankrupt trying to sell video game machines.
   The Cabbage Patch doll was a huge success.
   Coleco markets the Cabbage Patch doll.

   **(a)** The Cabbage Patch doll was a successful product for Coleco.
   **(b)** After failing with video game machines, Coleco was saved by the Cabbage Patch doll.
   **(c)** Coleco was unable to sell video game machines successfully.

2. AT&T's monopoly of long-distance service has ended.
   MCI and Sprint now offer long-distance telephone service.
   AT&T has had to lay off workers in order to remain competitive.

   **(a)** MCI and Sprint are the telephone companies of the future.
   **(b)** The ending of the AT&T telephone monopoly has led to competition and worker layoffs.
   **(c)** The AT&T telephone monopoly was in violation of anti-trust laws.

3. Hospital costs are higher than most people can afford.
   An unexpected illness can be a financial disaster for a family.
   Medical insurance pays for hospital costs and doctors' bills.

   **(a)** Medical insurance protects people from large health care bills.
   **(b)** The United States should adopt a National Health Insurance plan.
   **(c)** Medical costs are too high and should be reduced to help protect families.

**Answers start on page 199.**

# PUTTING THE DETAILS TOGETHER

## Topic and Main Idea

You have practiced finding, understanding, restating, and summarizing details so far in this chapter. The next step is to start putting these details together. To get a complete picture of what the writer is talking about, you must determine the topic and the main idea.

The **topic** is the subject of a passage. The **main idea** is the point the writer wants to make about the topic. The details provide evidence or examples or description to explain the main idea to you.

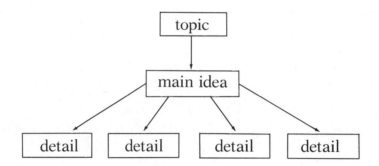

## Identifying the Topic

In the last exercise of the previous section, you summarized details and facts from three statements. You're now going to work with paragraphs. A **paragraph** is a group of sentences that help develop a central point or idea.

The topic is what the paragraph is about. One way to determine the topic of a paragraph is to look at the details. Study the details in the paragraph below. Do they suggest a topic, a subject that the whole paragraph relates to?

> The Federal Reserve controls the nation's money supply.
> Most people need to budget their money very carefully.
> Many products cater to young consumers. It is very hard to survive on welfare.

You probably are not sure what the topic of this group of sentences is. In fact, there is no single topic. These sentences look like a paragraph, but they are not. For a group of sentences to be a paragraph, they must be about a single topic.

The example that follows is a unified paragraph except for one thing: it contains a sentence that does not belong. Read the paragraph carefully. Decide what the topic of the paragraph is. Then identify the sentence that is not about the topic.

(1) These days many people do a lot of their banking by bank teller machine. (2) These bank teller machines can be found in many places, including department stores and supermarkets. (3) Banks supply their customers with access cards for the machines. (4) You can pay for groceries by check at many supermarkets. (5) Most bank teller machines can give you money from your account, tell you your account balance, or let you make a deposit.

▶ What is the topic of this paragraph? _____

▶ Which sentence does not belong? _____

The topic of this paragraph is bank teller machines. Each sentence is related to this topic except for sentence 4. Sentence 4 is about money, but it is not about bank teller machines.

## EXERCISE 9: IDENTIFYING UNRELATED SENTENCES

*Directions:* In each of the following paragraphs, one sentence does not belong. Read each paragraph carefully to find its topic. Then fill in the blank with the letter of the sentence that does not belong.

_____ 1. (a) Tanya bought a brand-new car. (b) Within six months the car had broken down eight times. (c) Under her state's "lemon" law, the car dealer had to replace the defective car. (d) Used car prices have gone up in recent years.

_____ 2. (a) Japanese products are very popular with American consumers. (b) For many years now, Americans have been buying a wide variety of these products, including cars, stereos, and VCRs. (c) The American automobile industry is making a comeback. (d) Now Japanese restaurants are becoming very popular in the United States. (e) Sushi, a Japanese dish, soon may be as well known to Americans as products made by Sony, a Japanese manufacturer.

_____ 3. (a) The Consumer Price Index (CPI) measures the inflation rate. (b) The cost of housing is a major factor in the CPI. (c) Food prices often depend on the weather. (d) Food and clothing costs are also major factors in the CPI. (e) As housing, food, and clothing costs rise, so does the Consumer Price Index.

_____ **4. (a)** One hundred years ago, most textiles used by Americans were made in the northeastern United States. **(b)** Then, looking for cheaper labor, many manufacturers moved to the southeastern United States. **(c)** In recent years, textile manufacturing has moved again. **(d)** Now the cheap labor is in eastern Asia, so most textiles are now made there. **(e)** Korea, Japan, Taiwan, and Hong Kong are all major trading partners with our country.

**Answers start on page 199.**

# Finding the Main Idea

Every paragraph has a topic, the subject of the paragraph. And every paragraph has a main idea. The ***main idea*** is the most important thing, or the central point, that the writer wants to say about the topic. Practice finding the topic and the main idea in the following example paragraph. Read the paragraph; then answer the questions that follow it.

> In our free enterprise system, anyone has the right to go into business. If you see a need, you do not have to have government permission to try to fill it. Whether it is a new computer company or a roadside fruit stand, you have the right to try to sell your products. And if you are successful, the rewards can be great.

▶ What is the topic of this paragraph? _____

▶ What do you think the writer's main point is? _____

_____

You were right if you said that the topic is "starting a business in our free enterprise system." Each sentence is related to this topic. The main idea is more specific than the topic. The main idea is stated in the first sentence, "In our free enterprise system, anyone has the right to go into business." This main idea tells you the central point of the rest of the sentences. You'll get more practice identifying the main idea on the following pages.

Now try another example. After the following paragraph are four choices for main idea. Circle the letter of the best choice for the main idea.

> Many of the world's developing countries have been spending more money than they make. They have borrowed money from large banks, including the World Bank. In the past decade, some of these countries, including Argentina, Mexico, and Brazil, have had trouble paying back their debts. As a result, the world economy is threatened by a debt crisis.

▸ What is the main idea of this paragraph?

    **(a)** Argentina is having trouble paying back its debts.
    **(b)** The world economy is threatened by a debt crisis.
    **(c)** Today, the world economy has made all countries interdependent.
    **(d)** The United States economy is the largest in the world.

You were correct if you chose (b). It sums up the central point of the paragraph. Choice (a) is too narrow because it is only a specific detail mentioned in the paragraph. Choice (c) is too broad and general. The main idea of this paragraph is more specific—*debt* in the world economy. Choice (d) is not mentioned in the passage at all.

## EXERCISE 10: IDENTIFYING THE MAIN IDEA

*Directions:* Following each paragraph are four choices for main idea. Put *M* by the main idea. Put *N* by the choice that is too narrow. Put *B* by the choice that is too broad. Put *X* by the choice that is not in the passage.

1. Children are a major target of television advertising. Some consumer groups are concerned about the results of targeting these young viewers. Exciting ads and magical promises can easily convince children that they must have the newest toy. Children then pressure their parents to buy toys that the family may not be able to afford. This problem can lead to overspending by the parents or very disappointed children.

    _____ **(a)** Television ads are usually aimed at a specific target group.
    _____ **(b)** Children are easily convinced by exciting TV ads that they must have the newest toy.
    _____ **(c)** Magazine ads aimed at teenagers could disrupt families.
    _____ **(d)** Consumer groups are concerned about the results of TV ads for children.

2. In a capitalist economy, most factories and farms are privately owned. In a socialist economy, the society as a whole owns the factories and the farms. Until recently, the Chinese had a socialist economy. But in recent years, the Chinese government has begun to experiment with private ownership. The Chinese are trying to combine the best of socialism and capitalism. In time, perhaps they will develop a completely new kind of economy.

    _____ **(a)** Capitalism and socialism are the two main economic systems in the world.
    _____ **(b)** China is experimenting with combining capitalism with socialism.
    _____ **(c)** China has successfully controlled the growth of its population.
    _____ **(d)** Most factories and farms are privately owned in a capitalist economy.

3. One measure of a healthy economy is the savings rate. The savings rate measures how much money people deposit in savings accounts. A savings account is a cushion against hard times. It is also a source of money for investment. In the United States, the savings rate is very low. Because of the low savings rate, the United States economy has less money available for investment and less protection against hard times than a country with a higher savings rate.

_____ **(a)** The low savings rate in the United States weakens the economy.

_____ **(b)** A savings account is a cushion against hard times.

_____ **(c)** The United States faces economic hard times.

_____ **(d)** Saving rates are important.

**Answers start on page 199.**

# Topic Sentences

As you have already seen, the main idea of a paragraph is sometimes stated directly in one of the sentences of the paragraph. This sentence is called the *topic sentence.* The topic sentence is often at the beginning of a paragraph. The topic sentence may also occur at the end or sometimes even in the middle of a paragraph. No matter where the topic sentence appears in the paragraph, all other sentences relate to it. They are *supporting* sentences—they support the main idea expressed in the topic sentence.

See if you can find the topic sentence in the following paragraph. If you can find the topic sentence, underline it.

> The Environmental Protection Agency (EPA) is responsible for the quality of our environment. The EPA enforces the Clean Water and Clean Air Acts. It must protect wetlands and other delicate ecosystems. In addition, toxic wastes and their disposal are the EPA's responsibility.

You were right if you underlined the first sentence. It introduces the main idea of the paragraph, that the EPA is responsible for the quality of the environment. The other three sentences all give examples of the EPA's responsibilities.

In the following example paragraph, the topic sentence has been replaced by a blank line. Read the paragraph carefully and answer the two questions below.

▶ What is the topic? _____

▶ What is the main point being made about the topic? _____

_____

Now write a topic sentence for the paragraph that expresses the main idea.

_____

_____ Only about half of all employees in the U.S. work a "standard" work week of thirty-five to forty-five hours. Almost a quarter of all employees work fewer than thirty-five hours. The rest work more than forty-five hours each week. However, experts think that these statistics don't tell the whole story. In reality, many of those thirty-five- to forty-five-hour workers may actually work much longer hours.

You were right if you said the topic of the paragraph is the number of hours people work each week. The writer's main point is that the forty-hour work week is probably not usual for U.S. workers. A good topic sentence for the paragraph might be something like this: *A forty-hour work week is probably not standard for most workers in the United States.*

## EXERCISE 11: WRITING TOPIC SENTENCES

*Directions:* In each of the following paragraphs, the topic sentence has been replaced by a blank line. Read the paragraph and answer the questions. Then, on the first line of the paragraph, write a topic sentence that introduces the main idea of the paragraph.

**1.** What is the topic? _____

What is the main point being made about the topic?

_____

_____

_____ The Federal Deposit Insurance Corporation (FDIC) was established in the 1930s after many people lost their life savings when banks failed. Today most bank accounts are insured by the FDIC up to a fixed amount. As a result, if a bank fails, the FDIC will replace money that depositors had in accounts at the failed bank.

**2.** What is the topic? _____

What is the main point being made about the topic?

_____

_____

_____ One common kind of consumer co-op is housing co-ops. Housing co-ops are owned jointly by the members who live in them. Another common type of consumer co-op is food co-ops. Food co-ops can be large supermarkets or small health-food stores. These co-ops are owned by the members who shop there. Child-care co-ops are preschools and day-care centers owned by members, the parents of the children who attend them.

**3.** What is the topic? _____

What is the main point being made about the topic?

_____

_____

_____ One of the problems Shirley had to face was how to pay for her increasing heating bills on her senior citizen's fixed income. She faced a similar problem with her phone bill. And finally she had to deal with the problem of rising property taxes. She was afraid that she would have to sell the house she had lived in for forty-five years.

**Answers start on page 199.**

# Finding the Main Idea of a Passage

The same process used in finding the main idea of a paragraph is used in finding the main idea of a passage. If you find the main idea of each paragraph in a passage, you will find that they are related. They all point to one overriding main idea for the passage as a whole. Read the following example passage. What is the main idea of the first paragraph? the second? the third? What is the one main idea that sums up the whole passage?

Before every presidential election, the Democratic and Republican parties hold statewide primary elections to find out which candidates draw the most votes. The New Hampshire primary election is the first state primary. Usually candidates who do well in this primary also do well across the country. So the New Hampshire primary is the candidate's first and perhaps best chance to impress the party and get the public's attention.

Though the New Hampshire primary is months away, the

campaign is off and running. Possible candidates from both parties are visiting the state to make campaign appearances. Republican Jack Kemp has already spent so much time here that campaign workers joke that he would qualify for state residency. Democrat Joseph Biden will be the guest of honor at the most important annual Democratic event in the state.

But there is more evidence of candidates' campaigning than just making speeches. Some likely candidates are giving money to political action committees to work in their behalf. And Senator Howard Baker is going to appoint a New Hampshire politician to run his presidential campaign. The candidates will try many strategies in hopes of running a good race in New Hampshire this year.

main idea of first paragraph: _____

_____

main idea of second paragraph: _____

_____

main idea of third paragraph: _____

_____

Did you fill in an answer close to the following ones for the main idea of each paragraph? The main idea of the first paragraph is that doing well in the New Hampshire primary is very important to presidential candidates. The main idea of the second paragraph is that candidates are starting to make campaign visits to the state. The main idea of the third paragraph is that the candidates will try many strategies in their New Hampshire campaigns.

Now you have looked at the main idea of each paragraph separately. But what about the passage as a whole? What is the main point the writer is trying to make? Look again at the main ideas for each of the three paragraphs. The main idea of the passage summarizes the main ideas of the individual paragraphs.

Write a main idea for the passage: _____

_____

_____

You might have written something like this:

Winning the New Hampshire primary is very important to presidential candidates, so they will be trying many strategies to win votes there.

Did the main idea you wrote contain all the important points?

## EXERCISE 12: MAIN IDEA OF A PASSAGE

*Directions:* Read the following passage. Then choose the correct main idea for each of the three paragraphs. Finally, choose the main idea for the passage.

**(1)** The Chicago Housing Authority (CHA) has decided to allow renters in one city housing project to manage the project themselves. The tenants of the LeClaire Courts complex have worked toward this decision for three years. They say that tenant management has made living conditions better in housing projects in other large cities.

**(2)** The new tenant managers will have almost complete control of their housing complex. They will take care of their own maintenance and security and select new tenants. In addition, the CHA has set aside $1 million for repairs in the complex. Residents will decide how the money will be spent. However, the tenant managers will report to the CHA's board of directors.

**(3)** LeClaire tenants have already formed a management company. A group of about fifteen tenants will be given an intensive three-month training program to learn to manage the housing project. Then they may have as much as two years' follow-up training. When their training period is over, the CHA will allow the tenant company to take over the complex.

1. The main idea of paragraph 1 is

   (a) the CHA is going to allow tenants of a housing project to manage it themselves
   (b) tenant management lowers the quality of life in housing projects
   (c) tenant management has succeeded in other major cities
   (d) LeClaire tenants have worked toward tenant management for three years

2. The main idea of paragraph 2 is

   (a) the CHA has set aside $1 million to repair the housing project
   (b) the CHA will decide how to use the repair money set aside for LeClaire Courts
   (c) the tenant managers will have almost complete control over LeClaire Courts
   (d) the tenant managers will have to report to the CHA's board of directors

**3.** The main idea of paragraph 3 is

   **(a)** the LeClaire tenants have formed a tenant management company
   **(b)** about 15 tenants will actually manage the complex
   **(c)** after tenant managers are trained, the tenant company will run the complex
   **(d)** the tenant managers will not need special training to manage the complex

**4.** Choose the sentence below that best summarizes the main idea of the entire passage you have just read. Use the main ideas of the individual paragraphs to help you choose the main idea of the passage.

   **(a)** Tenants lost their battle for control of the LeClaire Courts CHA housing project.
   **(b)** Following a training period, the CHA board will give a group of tenants almost complete control of their housing project.
   **(c)** Tenants will be deciding how to spend $1 million in rehab money at the CHA's LeClaire Courts development.
   **(d)** Tenant management has improved living conditions in public housing in several major cities.

**Answers start on page 199.**

## EXERCISE 13: CHAPTER REVIEW

*Directions:* Read the following passages and answer the questions, circling the number of the correct answer.

Questions 1–5 are based on the following passage.

> Harriet Hanson was an eleven-year-old girl working in the mill. She later recalled:
>
> I worked in a lower room where I had heard the proposed strike fully, if not vehemently, discussed. I had been an ardent listener to what was said against this attempt at "oppression" on the part of the corporation, and naturally I took sides with the strikers. When the day came on which the girls were to turn out, those in the upper rooms started first, and so many of them left that our mill was at once shut down. Then, when the girls in my room stood irresolute, uncertain what to do . . . I, who began to think they would not go out, after all their talk, became impatient, and started on ahead, saying with childish bravado, "I don't care what you do, I am going to turn out, whether anyone else does or not," and I marched out, and was followed by the others.
>
> As I looked back at the long line that followed me, I was more proud than I have ever been since. . . .

1. The topic of this passage is

   (1) a young girl growing up in a mill town
   (2) the tragedy of child labor
   (3) the rise of the labor movement
   (4) life in the early mills
   (5) a young girl's role in a mill strike

2. Harriet decided to *turn out*. This meant that

   (1) she rearranged her clothes
   (2) she went on strike
   (3) she told the other workers what to do
   (4) she went to the upper rooms
   (5) she converted to Catholicism

3. At first, the girls in Harriet's room stood *irresolute*. This meant that they

   (1) were embarrassed by Harriet
   (2) had decided to strike
   (3) had decided to stay at work
   (4) were uncertain about what to do
   (5) were older and wiser than Harriet

**4.** Harriet spoke with childish *bravado*. She showed

    **(1)** great confidence and maturity
    **(2)** pretended courage
    **(3)** a lack of responsibility
    **(4)** thoughtfulness
    **(5)** cowardice and fear

**5.** What happened when Harriet marched out of the mill?

    **(1)** She was immediately arrested.
    **(2)** She was fired from her job.
    **(3)** Her fellow workers followed her.
    **(4)** She was put in charge of the strike.
    **(5)** Her co-workers refused to talk to her.

Questions 6–7 are based on the following passage.

> It has long been true, and prisoners knew this better than anyone, that the poorer you were, the more likely you were to end up in jail. This was not just because the poor committed more crimes. In fact, they did. The rich did not have to commit crimes to get what they wanted; the laws were on their side. But when the rich did commit crimes, they often were not prosecuted, and if they were they could get out on bail, hire clever lawyers, get better treatment from judges. Somehow, the jails ended up full of poor black people.

**6.** According to the passage, why do the rich commit fewer crimes than the poor?

    **(1)** They have a better education than poor people.
    **(2)** They tend to be more religious than poor people.
    **(3)** They can get what they want since the law is on their side.
    **(4)** They can get out on bail, hire clever lawyers, get better treatment from judges.
    **(5)** They want to set a good example to others.

**7.** What is the main idea of this paragraph?

    **(1)** The poorer you are, the more likely you are to end up in jail.
    **(2)** Reform is needed to make the criminal justice system work.
    **(3)** Rich people can afford to hire clever lawyers and pay bail.
    **(4)** Poor people commit more crimes than rich people.
    **(5)** The criminal justice system must become tougher on criminals.

Questions 8–10 are based on the following passage.

In the spring of 1903, I went to Kensington, Pennsylvania, where seventy-five thousand textile workers were on strike. Of this number at least ten thousand were little children. The workers were striking for more pay and shorter hours. Every day little children came into Union Headquarters, some with their hands off, some with the thumb missing, some with their fingers off at the knuckle. They were stooped little things, round-shouldered and skinny. . . .

I asked some of the parents if they would let me have their little boys and girls for a week or ten days, promising to bring them back safe and sound. . . . A man named Sweeny was marshall. . . . A few men and women went with me. . . . The children carried knapsacks on their backs in which was a knife and fork, a tin cup and plate. . . . One little fellow had a drum, and another had a fife. . . . We carried banners that said: . . . "We want time to play. . . ."

. . .Our march had done its work. We had drawn the attention of the nation to the crime of child labor.

8. The children carried

   **(1)** eating utensils and musical instruments
   **(2)** knives and forks
   **(3)** the smaller children
   **(4)** more pay and shorter hours
   **(5)** a fife and drum

9. What is this passage about?

   **(1)** a children's march to protest child labor
   **(2)** an early fund-raising telethon
   **(3)** the right of children to play
   **(4)** the textile workers' strike in Kensington
   **(5)** the abuse and mutilation of children

10. How many textile workers were on strike in Kensington?

   **(1)** 10
   **(2)** 1,903
   **(3)** 7,000
   **(4)** 10,000
   **(5)** 75,000

**Answers start on page 200.**

## CHAPTER REVIEW EVALUATION CHART

| Reading Skill | Questions | Review Pages | Number Correct |
|---|---|---|---|
| Finding Details | 5, 6, 10 | 17–22 | _____ /3 |
| Words in Context | 2, 3, 4 | 22–27 | _____ /3 |
| Restating/ Summarizing | 8 | 27–31 | _____ /1 |
| Topic of a Passage | 1, 9 | 32–34 | _____ /2 |
| Main Idea of a paragraph | 7 | 34–36 | _____ /1 |

Your score: _____ out of 10

Passing score: 7 out of 10

# 2 Charts, Graphs, and Maps

Charts, graphs, and maps are often used in social studies materials. It is as important for you to understand these illustrations as it is for you to understand reading passages. Illustrations can give detailed information without many words, so they are very helpful to both readers and writers. Can you imagine what it would be like to read or to write the information on a road map in sentences and paragraphs?

Understanding charts, graphs, and maps will help you in future chapters of this book and in your daily life.

## CHARTS

### What Is a Chart?

A chart is information organized into columns and rows. The purpose of a chart is to allow you to easily locate and compare bits of information. The following example shows the major parts of a chart.

---

### EDUCATION COMPLETED, 1940-1980

Since 1940, the following percentage of Americans aged 25 or over had completed high school or college:

|  | High School Only | Four or More Years of College |
|---|---|---|
| 1940 | 24.5% | 4.6% |
| 1950 | 34.3% | 6.2% |
| 1960 | 41.4% | 7.7% |
| 1970 | 55.2% | 11.0% |
| 1980 | 66.3% | 16.3% |

Source: *U/S A Statistical Portrait of the American People*

---

In the chart above, the title gives the topic. A sentence below the title gives more information about the topic. The information, or **data**, on a chart is organized into rows and columns. A **row** of a chart is all the entries on one horizontal line. In the chart above, each row is labeled by a decade, such as 1940. A **column** consists of all the entries on one vertical line. In the chart above, there are two columns. The column headings are "High School Only" and "Four or More Years of College."

# Understanding a Chart

Just like a reading passage, every chart has a topic. The title usually tells you what a chart is about. You can often find more clues to the topic of a chart in the headings and sometimes in a subtitle. Look at the chart below.

What is this chart about? _____

---

### THE NATION'S LARGEST CITIES

| 1980 Rank | 1980 Population | Percentage Change Since 1970 |
|---|---|---|
| 1. New York | 7,015,608 | −11.1% |
| 2. Chicago | 2,969,570 | −11.9% |
| 3. Los Angeles | 2,950,010 | + 4.9% |
| 4. Philadelphia | 1,680,235 | −13.8% |
| 5. Houston | 1,554,992 | +26.1% |
| 6. Detroit | 1,192,222 | −21.3% |
| 7. Dallas | 901,450 | + 6.8% |

Source: *U/S A Statistical Portrait of the American People*

The chart is about the percent of population change in the nation's largest cities. You can figure this out by looking at the title and the headings for the columns and rows.

---

### Chart Reading Tip

In order to understand a chart, first read the title and all the headings. Don't try to read the data until you understand what the title and headings are telling you the chart is about.

---

## EXERCISE 1: READING THE TITLES AND HEADINGS ON A CHART

*Directions:* In your own words, write a sentence telling what each of the following charts is about.

**NATIONAL BASKETBALL ASSOCIATION STANDINGS**
**Atlantic Division**

|  | Wins | Losses | Percentage of Wins | Games Behind |
|---|---|---|---|---|
| Boston | 42 | 11 | .792 | — |
| Philadelphia | 36 | 20 | .643 | 7½ |
| New Jersey | 30 | 27 | .526 | 14 |
| Washington | 25 | 30 | .455 | 18 |
| New York | 19 | 37 | .339 | 24½ |

This chart is about _____

_____

**BOCES ADULT LEARNING CENTER**
**BUDGET ANALYSIS FOR FISCAL YEAR 1989**

| Budget Item | Amount Recommended |
|---|---|
| Salaries | $ 298,560 |
| Supplies | 12,490 |
| Equipment | 26,800 |
| Building | 48,000 |

This chart is about _____

_____

**Possible answers start on page 200.**

# Locating Data on a Chart

In order to find specific data (bits of information) on a chart, you must use the column and row headings to locate the information you need. The column and row headings label the vertical and horizontal lines of data. In the following chart, the column headings are *1970, 1980*, and *Percentage Change*. The row headings are the types of foods listed along the left side.

| CHANGES IN FOOD CONSUMPTION: 1970-1980 (Pounds per Person) | | | |
|---|---|---|---|
| | **1970** | **1980** | **Percentage Change** |
| Dairy products | 335.0 | 308.0 | −8.1% |
| Meat | 164.7 | 159.7 | −3.0% |
| Flour and cereal products | 142.0 | 150.0 | +5.6% |
| Fats and oils | 50.4 | 54.7 | +8.5% |
| Source: *U/S A Statistical Portrait of the American People* | | | |

The data in the chart above can be used to help us understand how the American diet changed from 1970 to 1980. Answer the following sample questions based on the chart.

▶ What was the number of pounds of meat consumed by the average American in 1980? _____

First look for the row labeled *Meat*. Then look for the column labeled *1980*. If you draw imaginary lines across from *Meat* and down from *1980*, the place where the lines cross is the number you are looking for. The average American ate 159.7 pounds of meat in 1980.

▶ Of the items listed, which food had the greatest percentage change in consumption from 1970 to 1980? _____

You must look for the largest number in the percentage change column. That number is +8.5%. Looking across the row, you find that fats and oils had the greatest percentage change of the items listed.

▶ Did the consumption of dairy products increase or decrease from 1970 to 1980? _____

To answer this question, you could compare two numbers. Consumption of dairy products for 1970 is 335.0. For 1980, it is 308.0. Since the 1980 number is lower, the consumption of dairy products decreased. You could also look in the "percentage change" column to find the answer to this question. The minus sign in that column tells you that consumption decreased.

▶ By how many pounds did the consumption of flour and cereal products increase from 1970 to 1980? _____

In order to find the amount of the increase, first find the amount of consumption in 1970 and in 1980. Consumption of flour and cereal products was 142.0 pounds in 1970 and 150.0 pounds in 1980. To find the increase, you need to find the difference between the two numbers, so you subtract: 150 − 142 = 8. Consumption increased by 8 pounds.

## Chart Reading Tip

If you are asked to find an increase, look for numbers or percentages that become larger over time. When you see a plus (+) sign, such as +18%, the plus sign tells you there was an increase of 18%. If you are asked to find a decrease, look for numbers that become smaller over time. When you see a minus (−) sign, such as −18%, the minus sign tells you there was a decrease of 18%.

## EXERCISE 2: FINDING INFORMATION ON A CHART

*Directions:* Use the information in the chart below to answer the questions at the top of page 51.

| CHANGES IN FOOD CONSUMPTION: 1970-1980 (Pounds per Capita) | | | |
|---|---|---|---|
| | 1970 | 1980 | Percentage Change |
| Fresh vegetables | 141.4 | 149.9 | + 6.0% |
| Sugar and other sweeteners | 121.4 | 133.4 | + 9.9% |
| Fresh fruits | 78.6 | 84.0 | + 6.9% |
| Poultry | 48.8 | 60.9 | +24.8% |
| Eggs | 39.2 | 34.6 | −11.7% |
| Fish | 15.8 | 16.8 | + 6.3% |
| Coffee, tea, and cocoa | 14.2 | 11.2 | −21.1% |
| All foods | 1,402.0 | 1,408.0 | + 0.4% |
| All animal products | 619.0 | 592.0 | − 4.4% |
| All crop products | 783.0 | 816.0 | + 4.2% |

1. How many pounds of eggs were consumed by the average American in 1970? _____

2. In 1980, the average American ate 16.8 pounds of what food item? _____

3. What food item had the greatest percentage increase in consumption from 1970 to 1980? _____

4. Between 1970 and 1980, did the consumption of all animal products increase or decrease? _____

5. By what percentage did the consumption of all foods increase between 1970 to 1980? _____

6. Americans cut back their consumption of many food items from 1970 to 1980. What category decreased by the greatest percentage? _____

**Answers start on page 200.**

# Finding the Main Idea of a Chart

Like a reading passage, a chart may illustrate a main idea. The author may be trying to make a central point by choosing and displaying data a certain way. When you study a chart, ask yourself what the chart is telling you and what its purpose is. Then think of a way the data could be summarized in one main idea statement.

Sometimes the main idea of a chart will be stated directly in the title or subtitle. Other times you must find the main idea by looking at the headings or by studying the data.

---

### Chart Reading Tip

Because data are easier to read and compare in smaller numbers, charts that compare large numbers will often use phrases like *in thousands* in their subtitle or key. *In thousands* means that each number listed in the chart is really 1,000 times that number. So, for example, the number *18* on a chart that says *in thousands* actually means *18,000*.

| GAINERS AND LOSERS<br>Union membership in thousands | | | |
|---|---|---|---|
| | 1965 | 1975 | 1985 |
| United Steel Workers | 876 | 1,062 | 572 |
| International Ladies' Garment Workers Union | 363 | 363 | 210 |
| Communications Workers of America | 288 | 476 | 524 |
| United Automobile Workers | 1,150 | n.a. | 974 |
| Service Employees International Union | 305 | 480 | 688 |

Source: *The New York Times*/AFL-CIO

Study the chart "Gainers and Losers." Read the title, subtitle, and headings. Then look carefully at the data to see what the chart is illustrating. Ask yourself what the chart is telling you and what its purpose could be.

Following are four choices for the main idea. Circle the number of the choice that accurately summarizes the data for the chart. What is the main idea of this chart?

**(1)** The largest unions have thousands of members.
**(2)** In the last ten years, the United Steel Workers Union lost almost half its members.
**(3)** While most unions lost members over the last twenty years, some have gained members.
**(4)** In life, there are always gainers and losers.

You were correct if you circled (3). Of the five unions listed, three have lost members over the last twenty years, while two have gained members. The chart makes clear that the "gainers and losers" are the different unions.

While choice (1) is a true statement that is supported by the data, it is not the main point of the chart, which shows the *changes* in union membership over time. Choice (2) is also a detail, not the main idea. Choice (4) is a general statement that does not refer to the data at all.

## EXERCISE 3: MAIN IDEA OF A CHART

*Directions:* After each chart are five choices for main idea. Choose the one that accurately summarizes the data on the chart.

| EARNINGS: SEX AND OCCUPATIONS | | | |
|---|---|---|---|
| For every $1,000 made by men in these occupations during 1981, women received the following amounts. | | | |
| Postal clerks | $939 | Cooks | $734 |
| Cashiers | $920 | Waiters and waitresses | $720 |
| Security guards | $907 | Accountants | $712 |
| Bartenders | $844 | Bookkeepers | $694 |
| Elementary school teachers | $822 | Manufacturing assemblers | $690 |
| Nursing aides and orderlies | $822 | Office machine operators | $688 |
| Stock handlers | $812 | Sales clerks | $674 |
| Social workers | $799 | Insurance agents | $671 |
| Cleaning service workers | $756 | Office managers | $655 |
| Computer programmers | $736 | Blue-collar supervisors | $642 |

Source: *U/S A Statistical Portrait of the American People*

1. What is the main idea of this chart?

   **(1)** More women are working than ever before.
   **(2)** Throughout a broad range of job categories, women earn less than men in the same occupation.
   **(3)** Postal clerk is the occupation in which women come closest to wage equality with men.
   **(4)** Blue-collar supervisor is the occupation in which women are paid the least compared to men.
   **(5)** A woman's place is in the home.

| UNDERGRADUATE DEGREES AWARDED TO WOMEN | | | |
|---|---|---|---|
| | 1971–1972 | 1979–1980 | Percentage Change |
| Engineering | 1.0% | 9.3% | +830.0% |
| Agriculture | 5.5% | 29.1% | +429.1% |
| Business | 9.7% | 33.7% | +247.4% |
| Computer science | 13.6% | 30.3% | +122.8% |
| Psychology | 46.4% | 70.4% | + 51.7% |
| Social sciences | 36.3% | 43.7% | + 20.4% |
| Education | 74.1% | 73.9% | − 0.3% |

Source: *U/S A Statistical Portrait of the American People*

2.   What is the main idea of this chart?

(1)   By the late 1970s, women were generally earning a greater percentage of undergraduate degrees in the fields listed.

(2)   An increasing number of women are getting degrees in engineering.

(3)   Women are going after men's jobs.

(4)   Women obtained higher salaries in 1979–80 than they did in 1971–72.

(5)   Despite a small decline, education is still the most female-dominated undergraduate degree.

**Answers start on page 200.**

# GRAPHS

A graph allows a reader to spot trends, make comparisons, and draw conclusions from data. Being able to read graphs will help you in many practical situations as well as in social studies. In this part of the chapter, you will look at four types of graphs: pictographs, bar graphs, line graphs, and circle graphs.

## Finding the Topic of a Graph

Like a chart, every graph has a topic. The title usually tells you the topic of the graph. Sometimes there is also a subtitle to help you out. Read the titles, then check the other information on the graph, such as the labels and the data, to make sure you have an accurate idea of the topic of the graph. Look at the sample graph below. What is the topic of this graph?

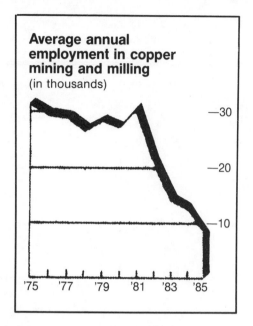

This graph shows the average annual employment in copper mining and milling. The title of this graph tells you what the graph is about.

## EXERCISE 4: TOPIC OF A GRAPH

*Directions:* In the space provided, write the topic of the following graphs. Study the titles and other information on each graph carefully before writing.

Graph 1

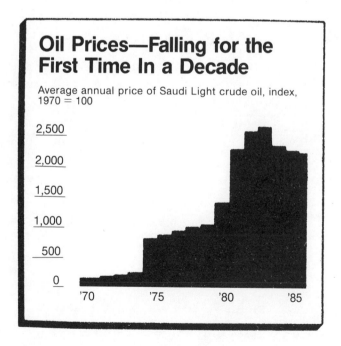

topic: _____

Graph 2

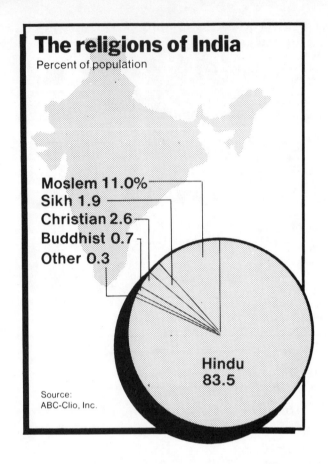

topic: _____

**Possible answers start on page 201.**

# The Main Idea of a Graph

Graphs illustrate a point. Usually the main idea will be stated directly in the title or subtitle. To determine the main idea, read the titles and other written information and look at the data. Ask yourself, "What message is the graph giving me?" Then think of a way to summarize the information.

Study the graph on page 57. Read the title, the scale, and the labels and look at the data. Then answer the questions that follow it. (The abbreviation *Mass.* on the graph stands for *Massachusetts.*)

## UNEMPLOYMENT RATE—1985
### (in percent)

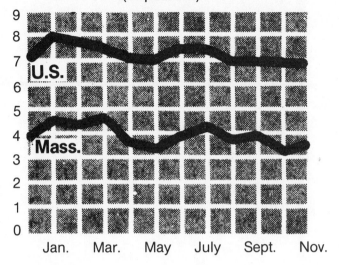

1. What is the graph about? _____

2. Why are there two lines on the graph? _____

3. The main idea of this graph is

   **(1)** the Massachusetts unemployment rate was consistently below the national average
   **(2)** the unemployment rate in the United States peaked at 8% and then dropped slightly
   **(3)** the unemployment rate in Massachusetts dipped as low as 3%
   **(4)** Massachusetts's high school dropout rate is lower than the national average
   **(5)** Massachusetts had the lowest unemployment rate in the nation

Be sure you tried to answer all the questions above. Then read the following explanations of the correct answers.

1. The topic of the graph is *1985 unemployment rates in the United States and Massachusetts.* You know this by looking at the title and the labels for the two lines.

2. There are two lines because two things are being compared. One line stands for the United States as a whole, and the other line stands for the state of Massachusetts.

3. Choice (1) is correct because it describes the relationship between the two lines. Choices (2) and (3) deal with only one of the two lines. Choice (4) has nothing to do with the graph. Choice (5) is related to the graph, but the graph does not show data for other states.

## EXERCISE 5: THE MAIN IDEA OF A GRAPH

*Directions:* This exercise is based on two graphs. Before you answer any of the questions about a graph, read the titles and the other written information and look at the data. Ask yourself what message the graph might be trying to give you and what its purpose might be.

After each graph are "warm-up" questions to help you understand the graph and then five choices for main idea. Answer the "warm-up" questions in your own words. Then choose the number of the correct choice for the main idea of each graph.

# RISING HOSPITAL COSTS

*According to the Health Insurance Association of America, average Cost To Hospitals Per Patient Stay of 7.6 days*

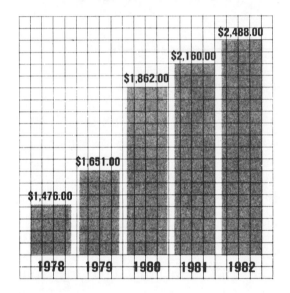

1. What is the topic of this graph? _____

   _____

2. What trend do you see when you look at the height of the bars changing over time? (A trend is a general direction or pattern of development.)

   _____

3. What is the main idea of the graph?

   **(1)** The rate of increase of hospital costs is slowing down.
   **(2)** Hospital costs increased each year between 1978 and 1982.
   **(3)** Hospital costs peaked in 1982.
   **(4)** The high cost of a hospital stay makes health insurance a necessity.
   **(5)** High hospital costs are a national scandal.

**PERSONAL BUDGET OF A
TYPICAL WELFARE RECIPIENT**

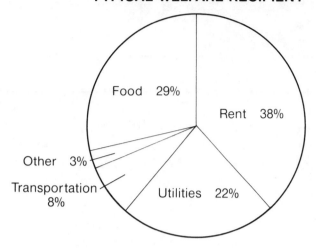

**4.** What is the topic of this graph? _____

_____

**5.** The graph shows that, in general, welfare recipients spend most of

their money on three things. What are they? _____

_____

**6.** What is the main idea of this graph?

    **(1)** Welfare recipients spend a great deal of their income on rent.
    **(2)** Welfare reform is long overdue.
    **(3)** Welfare recipients spend most of their money on necessities.
    **(4)** Welfare recipients do not manage their money wisely.
    **(5)** When people have to spend most of their income on food, rent,
        and energy, they go on welfare.

**Answers start on page 201.**

# READING DATA ON A GRAPH

## Finding Information on a Pictograph

A *pictograph* uses symbols to display information. In order to find specific details on a pictograph, you must use the **key**. The key tells you what the pictures on the graph stand for. For example, look at the following pictograph. Each picture, or symbol, stands for 50 prisoners per 100,000 people. Find the number of prisoners per 100,000 people in Delaware.

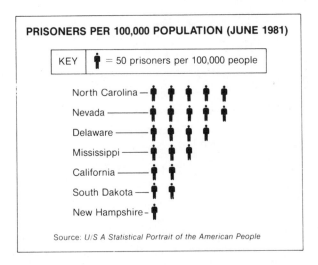

Find the row labeled *Delaware*. There are four symbols. The key tells you that each symbol stands for 50 prisoners. Multiply: $4 \times 50 = 200$. There are about 200 prisoners per 100,000 people in Delaware.

Look again at the pictograph in the example and answer the following questions.

▶ Which states had the highest number of prisoners per 100,000 people? _____

To find the states with the highest number of prisoners per 100,000 people, you must find the longest rows of symbols. Those rows are labeled *North Carolina* and *Nevada*.

▶ Which state had the lowest number of prisoners per 100,000 people? _____

To find the state with the lowest number of prisoners per 100,000 people, you must find the shortest row. That row is labeled *New Hampshire*.

▶ Which state has more prisoners per 100,000 population, Mississippi or California? _____

Mississippi has more. Mississippi's row has three symbols, and California's has only two.

## Graph Reading Tip
Pictographs are used to make general comparisons. The information on a pictograph is not exact.

# EXERCISE 6: READING PICTOGRAPHS

*Directions:* Fill in the blanks with the correct information based on each graph.

**CITY TAXES PER PERSON**

Key | **$** = $100

New York —————— $  $  $  $  $  $  $  $

San Antonio —————— $

San Francisco —————— $  $  $  $

Washington, D.C.— $  $  $  $  $  $  $  $  $  $
                      $  $  $

New Orleans —————— $  $

Source: *U/S A Statistical Portrait of the American People*

1. What were the approximate taxes per person in New Orleans? _____

2. Which city had the highest taxes per person? _____

3. Which city had the lowest taxes per person? _____

4. Which city's per-person taxes are lower, San Francisco's or New York's? _____

5. What is the main idea of the pictograph "City Taxes per Person"?

    **(1)** Washington, D.C., is one of the most expensive cities in the country to live in.
    **(2)** San Antonio and New Orleans have very low city taxes.
    **(3)** Cities that bring in a lot of tax money are able to provide more services to the public.
    **(4)** Per-person city taxes in the United States can range from as little as $100 to as much as $1,300.
    **(5)** City taxes in San Francisco are reasonable, so most people could afford to live there.

**Answers start on page 201.**

# Reading Bar Graphs

A *bar graph* uses bars to display information. Like a pictograph, a bar graph is a way to compare information quickly and easily. The information is not exact, but you can make good estimates from a bar graph. Study the following bar graph. In order to find specific facts on a bar graph, you must use the scale to read the height of the bars. What is the average life expectancy for women in the United States?

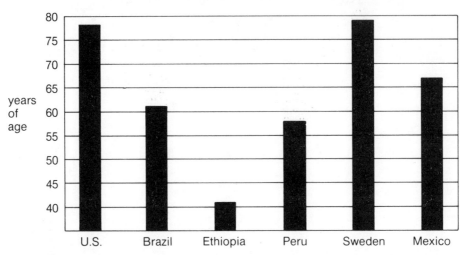

**AVERAGE LIFE EXPECTANCY FOR WOMEN—1980**

Source: *The New State of the World Atlas*

In order to find the average life expectancy for women in the United States, first you must find the bar labeled *U.S.* Now draw an imaginary horizontal line from the top end of the bar over to the scale. Then either read the number on the scale or, if the line is between two scale entries, estimate the number. In this case, the average life expectancy of women in the U.S. is between 75 and 80.

Use the bar graph in the example above to answer the following questions.

▶ What nation had the shortest life expectancy for women? _____

To find the nation with the shortest life expectancy, find the shortest bar. At the bottom of the bar is the name of the country, Ethiopia.

▶ Only one nation on the graph had a life expectancy for women similar to that of the U.S. What was that country? _____

To find the nation with a life expectancy similar to that of the U.S., find the U.S. bar. Now draw an imaginary horizontal line across the graph even with the top end of the U.S. bar. You will find that only one other bar ends near the line. At the bottom of that bar is the name of the country, Sweden.

### Graph Reading Tip

In multiple-choice questions based on graphs, you can eliminate wrong choices. Since you are usually expected to make estimates based on graphs, there should be one answer choice that is closest to your estimate.

## EXERCISE 7: READING BAR GRAPHS

*Directions:* Fill in the blanks with the correct information from the graph. Estimate the answer if you cannot read an exact figure from the graph.

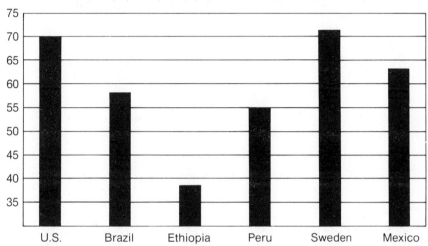

AVERAGE LIFE EXPECTANCY FOR MEN—1980

Source: *The New State of the World Atlas*

1. What nation had an average life expectancy for men of sixty-three years? _____

2. What was the average life expectancy for men in Peru? _____

3. What nation had the longest life expectancy for men?

_____

4. What nation had the shortest life expectancy for men?

_____

5. How many nations on the graph had a shorter life expectancy for men than the United States? _____

6. About how many more years does the average man in Sweden live than the average man in Ethiopia? _____

**Answers start on page 201.**

# Reading Line Graphs

A *line graph* is similar to a bar graph in many ways. However, instead of using bars, lines connect different points (called *data points*). Line graphs are used to show trends or developments. On the side of a line graph is a **vertical scale**. Along the bottom of a line graph is a **horizontal scale**. To read a line graph, you read up from the horizontal scale and across from the vertical scale to a particular point on the line.

Line graphs are easier to understand if you carefully read the titles and other words on the graph before you try reading the data. Study the following line graph and answer the question, "What was the population of London in 1800?"

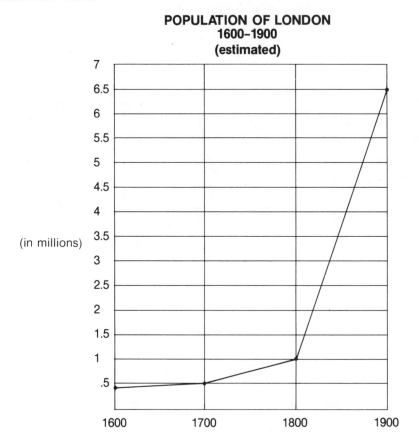

**POPULATION OF LONDON
1600–1900
(estimated)**

(in millions)

In order to find the population of London in 1800, first find *1800* on the horizontal scale (along the bottom of the graph). Now go straight up until you reach the data point for 1800. Now go straight across to the left until you reach the vertical scale. At the height of the data point, the closest number on the vertical scale is 1. That means that the population of London in 1800 was about 1 million.

Use the line graph in the example above to answer the following questions.

▶ In what year shown on the graph did London have the smallest population? _____

Find the lowest data point on the line. Look straight down to the horizontal scale and find the date of that point. London had its smallest population in 1600.

▶ In what year shown on the graph did London have its largest population? _____

Look at the line and find the highest point on it. Looking down to the horizontal scale, you find the year 1900. Therefore, London had its largest population in 1900.

▶ Between 1600 and 1900, what happened to the size of London's population? _____

Look at the first point on the line, the shape of the line, and the endpoint of the line. The population of London increased greatly during the period, from less than half a million people to 6.5 million.

To summarize or see a trend on a line graph, look at the whole line and get a general idea of what happened to the data over the time shown.

## EXERCISE 8: READING LINE GRAPHS

*Directions:* Answer the questions based on the following graph. If you can't read an exact answer from the graph, estimate.

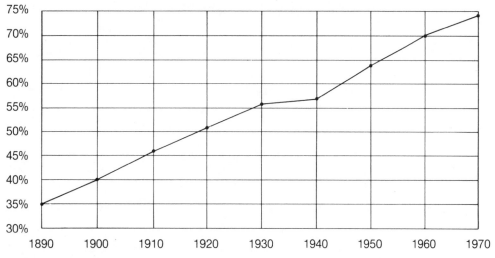

**AMERICA MOVES TO THE CITIES**
**Percent of U.S. Population Living in Urban Areas**

Source: *U/S A Statistical Portrait of the American People*

1. In what year shown on the graph was the percentage of urban population the lowest? _____

2. In what year shown on the graph was the percentage of urban population the highest? _____

3. What percentage of the population of the United States lived in urban areas in 1960? _____

**4.** Which of the following best describes the trend shown by this line graph?

  **(1)** The percentage of people living in urban areas of the United States has steadily fallen.
  **(2)** The percentage of people living in rural areas of the United States has steadily increased.
  **(3)** The percentage of people living in a few major cities in the United States has risen steadily.
  **(4)** In 1890, most people lived in the northeastern United States, but by 1980 the population was shifting south and west.
  **(5)** The percentage of people living in urban areas of the United States has risen steadily.

**Answers start on page 201.**

# Reading Circle Graphs

A circle graph uses parts, or segments, of a circle to display information. Think of the circle graph as a pie. The segments look like slices of the pie. The size of the segment tells how much of the whole it represents.

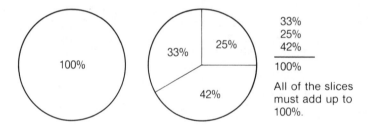

On the following graph, each segment has a label to tell you what it stands for. Find what percent of the U.S. population earned between $15,000 and $20,000.

**DISTRIBUTION OF FAMILY INCOME—1980**

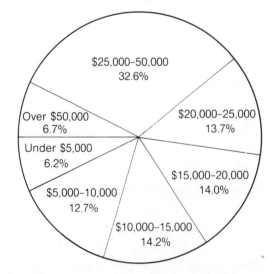

Source: *U/S A Statistical Portrait of the American People*

First find the segment labeled *$15,000–$20,000*. The percentage *14.0%* is written just below the label of the segment. Sometimes the label and percentage are written in the segment. Other times, especially when the segment is very small, they may be connected to the segment by a line.

Use the circle graph "Distribution of Family Income" to answer the following sample questions.

▶ The largest percentage of families in 1980 were at what income level? _____

Find the largest segment—32.6%. It is labeled *$25,000–50,000*.

▶ In 1980, 12.7% of families were at what income level? _____

Look for the segment marked *12.7%*. Read the label of that segment: *$5,000–10,000*.

## EXERCISE 9: READING CIRCLE GRAPHS
*Directions:* Fill in the blanks with the correct information based on each graph.

**THE STATE BUDGET**

Where the money goes

- Education 7.8%
- General government 3.7%
- Debt service 5.8%
- Economic development 4.3%
- Criminal justice and public safety 5.2%
- Local aid 28.7%
- Income support 23.1%
- Other human services 21.4%

1. What percent of the state budget pays for education?

    _____

2. In what area does the state government spend the most money?

    _____

3. What expense uses up exactly 4.3% percent of the state budget?

    _____

4. Does the state spend more money on education or on criminal justice and public safety? _____

**POPULATION BY AGE GROUP IN THE CITY OF SADDLETOP**

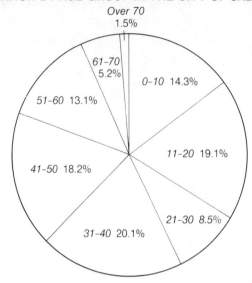

**5.** What age group makes up the smallest percentage of the population?

_____

**6.** What age group makes up the largest percentage of the population?

_____

**7.** What age group below 60 makes up the smallest percentage of the population? _____

**8.** Which age group is larger, the 11-20 group or the 41-50 group?

_____

**Answers start on page 201.**

# READING MAPS

## What Are Maps?

"Excuse me, sir, could you help me find 838 Catalpa Drive?"

"No problem. Just continue up Franklin Avenue and make a right at the gas station. You will then be on Woodcliff Drive. One block up, the road forks. Take the left fork. You are now on Shelburne Drive. Continue on Shelburne until you bear right at the next fork . . ."

"I'm sorry. You've lost me. I just can't picture where I'm supposed to be going."

"Let me draw you a map. Then it should be clearer."

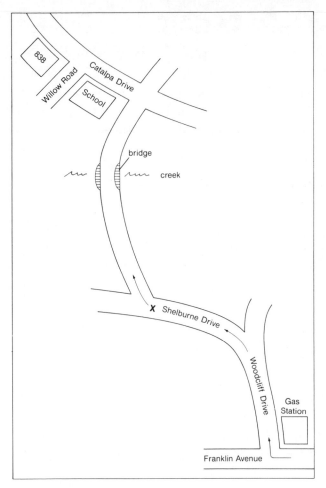

It is easier to follow directions when you use a map. See if you can find the gas station described in the directions. Now find the fork on Woodcliff Drive where Shelburne Drive splits off. Follow Shelburne Drive to where it forks.

Use the map to finish writing directions to 838 Catalpa Drive. Start at the *X* on the map and use landmarks whenever you can.

_____

_____

Your directions should be something like this: Take the right fork. Go straight over a bridge above a small creek. On your left you will see a school. Turn left at the school. You will then be on Catalpa Drive. Continue on Catalpa Drive past Willow Road. On the left you'll find 838 Catalpa Drive.

A ***map*** is a drawing of the surface of a region. A map could represent the entire earth, a continent, or a nation. Or, as in the above example, it can represent an area as small as your own neighborhood.

There are different kinds of maps for different purposes. In this chapter, you will be looking at common parts of maps, including directions, distances, keys, and borders between states and countries. You will then be able to practice reading different kinds of maps.

# Direction and Distance

Different kinds of information are found on a map. There are important symbols on a map that help orient us to it and see how the places shown on a map fit together. Following is a map of the Baltimore area. The direction symbol in the upper right corner of the map shows that the top of the map is north. This means that places near the top of the map are north of things lower down on the map. If you know north you can figure out the other directions.

If north is toward the top of the map, south is toward the bottom. East is to the right, and west is to the left.

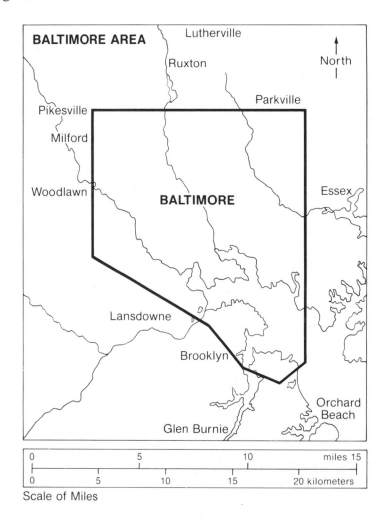

Scale of Miles

▶ Lutherville is straight north of Baltimore. Name a town that is straight east of Baltimore. _____

East is to the right. Therefore, look to the right of Baltimore. The town of Essex is east of Baltimore.

At the bottom of the map is a *scale* in miles. You can use the scale to estimate distances. The easiest way to use a scale of miles is to mark off the distance between two places on the edge of a piece of paper. Then put the edge of the paper next to the scale of miles to estimate the distance.

▶ About how many miles is it from Baltimore's west boundary near Woodlawn directly across town to its east boundary? _____

On the edge of a piece of paper, mark off the distance from the west boundary near Woodlawn straight across to the east boundary. Now line up the left marking for the west boundary with the zero on the scale at the bottom of the map. Your right marking for the east boundary should hit the scale at a little less than 10 miles. Now you know it is a little less than 10 miles from the west boundary to the east boundary of Baltimore.

## EXERCISE 10: DIRECTION AND DISTANCE ON A MAP

*Directions:* Answer the following questions based on the map of Cambodia.

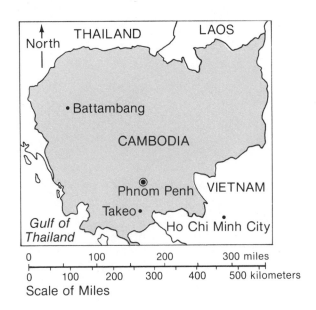

1. What two nations are north of Cambodia?

   _____

2. What direction must you travel to go from Phnom Penh to

   Takeo? _____

3. Approximately how many miles is it from Battambang to Phnom

   Penh? _____

4. If you travel south from Battambang, what body of water will you

   reach? _____

5. Approximately how many miles is it from Phnom Penh to Ho Chi

   Minh City in Vietnam? _____

**Answers start on page 202.**

# Using a Map Key

Most maps have keys. A map key defines the various symbols used on a map. A key can define different kinds of boundary lines such as international and state boundaries. It can give symbols for cities of varying sizes and for capital cities. It can identify symbols that represent vegetation, climate, population, and economic products.

The following is a map of New England, a region in the northeastern United States. Look at the key to find the symbol for state capitals.

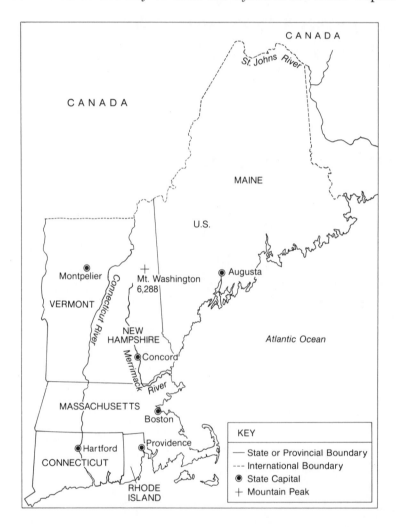

▶ What is the state capital of Connecticut? _____

Looking at the key, you find that ◉ is the symbol for state capitals. Find the state of Connecticut on the map. Now look for the symbol ◉ within the state. The symbol is labeled Hartford, which is the capital of Connecticut.

Look again at the key to determine what kind of line is used for the international boundary between Canada and the United States.

▶ What river is part of that international boundary? _____

The key tells you that the international boundary is marked by a dotted line.

Following the dotted line, only one river is part of that boundary, the St. Johns River between Maine and Canada.

▶ The only mountain peak marked on this map is Mt. Washington, the highest peak in New England. In what state is Mt. Washington located? _____

The key tells you that the symbol for a mountain is +. Looking for the symbol + on the map, you should be able to locate Mt. Washington, which is in the state of New Hampshire.

## EXERCISE 11: USING A MAP KEY

*Directions:* Brazil is one of the largest countries in the world. It is in South America. Use the map of Brazil to answer the following questions. For some of the questions, you will have to use the key.

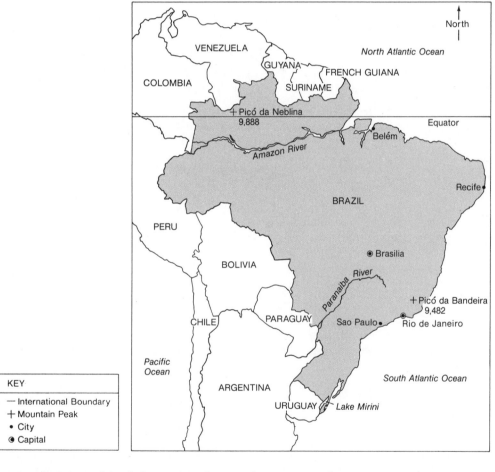

1. A major geographical feature of Brazil is a very famous river that runs across the northern part of the country. What is the name of the river? _____

2. Part of the southernmost tip of Brazil is a lake. What is the name of the lake? _____

**3.** With what other country does Brazil share the lake at its southern

tip? _____

**4.** What is the capital of Brazil? _____

**5.** The mouth of a river is where it enters the ocean. The mouth of the Amazon River is near what special line that crosses the

map? _____

**6.** What is the name of the highest mountain peak in

Brazil? _____

**Answers start on page 202.**

# Historical Maps

Historical maps can help us understand the past. They can show political boundaries of a past time period. They also can be used to illustrate historical trends and events. Sometimes these maps of the past can also help us make sense of the present. Look at the following map of the eastern United States before the American Revolution. What nation controlled the Great Lakes and the region around them?

**COLONIAL AMERICA**

In order to find what nation controlled the Great Lakes area, first find the Great Lakes on the map. The area north and east of the Great Lakes is called *New France*. The area south and west of the lakes is called *French Louisiana*. So you know that the whole region was controlled by France.

Look again at the map of the thirteen colonies on page 74 and answer the following questions.

▶ What nation controlled New York (N.Y.)? _____

Find New York (N.Y.) on the map. It was one of the thirteen colonies controlled by Great Britain.

▶ What nation controlled Florida? _____

Florida was called *Spanish Florida,* so you know it was controlled by Spain.

## EXERCISE 12: READING HISTORICAL MAPS

Answer the questions based on the following map.

**NATIVE AMERICANS OF NORTH AMERICA**

1. The Pawnee were part of which group of Native Americans?

    **(1)** Eskimo and Aleut
    **(2)** Eastern Forests Indians
    **(3)** Plains Indians
    **(4)** Northwest Coast Indians
    **(5)** Southwest Indians

**2.** The far north of the continent was inhabited by which group or groups?

    **(1)** Eskimo and Aleut
    **(2)** Eastern Forests Indians
    **(3)** Plains Indians
    **(4)** Northwest Coast Indians
    **(5)** Southwest Indians

**3.** Which of the following tribes was Southwest Indians?

    **(1)** Cree
    **(2)** Paiute
    **(3)** Cherokee
    **(4)** Sioux
    **(5)** Hopi

**Answers start on page 202.**

## EXERCISE 13: CHAPTER REVIEW

*Directions:* Study each illustration carefully, then choose the correct answer.

Questions 1–3 are based on the following chart.

| NUMBER OF ABORTIONS PER 1,000 BIRTHS: 1979 (entire U.S. = 358 per 1,000) | | | |
|---|---|---|---|
| New York | 666 | Texas | 290 |
| California | 515 | Ohio | 255 |
| Florida | 465 | Arizona | 171 |
| Pennsylvania | 407 | Mississippi | 96 |
| Tennessee | 324 | Wyoming | 84 |

Source: *U/S A Statistical Portrait of the American People*

1. Which of the states listed in the chart had the lowest number of abortions per 1,000 births in 1979?

   (1) New York
   (2) California
   (3) Tennessee
   (4) Texas
   (5) Wyoming

2. How many abortions for every 1,000 births were there in New York in 1979?

   (1) 358
   (2) 666
   (3) 84
   (4) 1,000
   (5) 324

3. Which of the following states had an abortion rate lower than that of the U.S. overall?

   (1) New York
   (2) California
   (3) Florida
   (4) Pennsylvania
   (5) Tennessee

Questions 4–5 are based on the following pictograph.

**LEADING CATTLE COUNTRIES**
**Number of Beef and Dairy Cattle in 1979**

India
181,849,000 (estimated)

Soviet Union
114,086,000

United States
110,864,000

Brazil
90,000,000

China
63,718,000

Argentina
60,174,000

Bangladesh
31,741,000

Mexico
29,920,000

Australia
27,107,000

Colombia
26,137,000

Sources: U.S. Department of Agriculture; FAO.

**4.** Which nation had the most beef and dairy cattle in 1979?

**(1)** India
**(2)** United States
**(3)** Colombia
**(4)** Canada
**(5)** Argentina

**5.** Which nation ranks third in total number of beef and dairy cattle in 1979?

**(1)** India
**(2)** United States
**(3)** Colombia
**(4)** Canada
**(5)** Argentina

Questions 6–7 are based on the following bar graph.

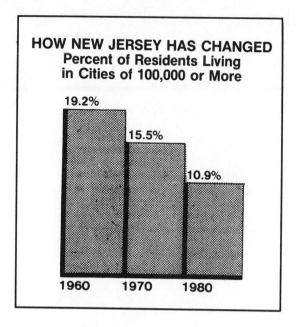

**6.** What is the main idea of this bar graph?

(1) New Jersey has changed.
(2) A declining number of Americans live in cities of over 100,000.
(3) New Jersey's population declined between 1960 and 1980.
(4) An increasing percentage of New Jersey residents live in cities of 100,000 or more.
(5) The percentage of New Jersey residents living in cities of 100,000 or more declined between 1960 and 1980.

**7.** What percent of New Jersey residents lived in cities of 100,000 or more in 1970?

(1) 19.2%
(2) 18.3%
(3) 15.5%
(4) 10.9%
(5) 7.2%

Questions 8–9 are based on the following line graph.

### USA TODAY VS. THE COMPETITION
### Paid Circulation

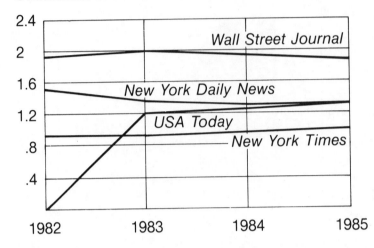

Source: *Boston Globe*/Audit Bureau of Circulations

8. Which two papers had the same circulation in 1985?

   **(1)** *New York Times* and *USA Today*
   **(2)** *Wall Street Journal* and *New York Daily News*
   **(3)** *New York Times* and *Wall Street Journal*
   **(4)** *USA Today* and *Wall Street Journal*
   **(5)** *New York Daily News* and *USA Today*

9. What was the circulation of the *Wall Street Journal* at the beginning of 1983?

   **(1)** 1,200
   **(2)** 2,000
   **(3)** 2,400
   **(4)** 2,000,000
   **(5)** 2,400,000

Questions 10–12 are based on the following circle graph.

### HOW STUDENTS WHO LIVE AT HOME
### TRAVEL TO SCHOOL
### Grades 1-6

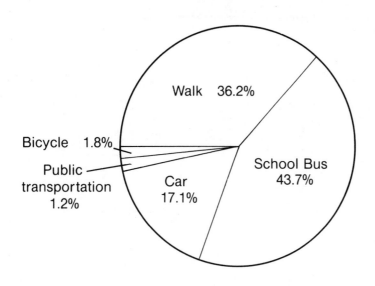

Source: *U/S A Statistical Portrait of the American People*

10. The main idea of this circle graph is

    **(1)** most Americans oppose school busing
    **(2)** nobody walks to school anymore
    **(3)** most elementary school children ride a school bus to school regularly
    **(4)** most children in grades 1–6 get to school by walking, school bus, or car
    **(5)** bicycles are becoming more popular for traveling to school

11. What percent of children in grades 1–6 travel to school by car?

    **(1)** 1.2%
    **(2)** 1.8%
    **(3)** 17.1%
    **(4)** 36.2%
    **(5)** 43.7%

12. 43.7 percent of students in grades 1-6 travel to school by what means?

    **(1)** walk
    **(2)** school bus
    **(3)** car
    **(4)** bicycle
    **(5)** public transportation

Questions 13–14 are based on the following map.

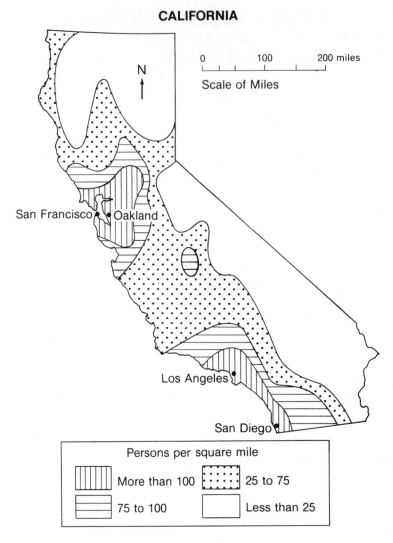

**CALIFORNIA**

13. What is the population density of the area within 25 miles of San Francisco?

    (1) less than 10
    (2) less than 25
    (3) 25 to 75
    (4) 75 to 100
    (5) more than 100

14. If you drove 200 miles straight north from San Diego and stopped, what would be the population density of the area you stopped in?

    (1) less than 25
    (2) 25 to 75
    (3) 75 to 100
    (4) more than 100
    (5) more than 500

Questions 15–17 are based on the following map.

**THE UNION AND THE CONFEDERACY**

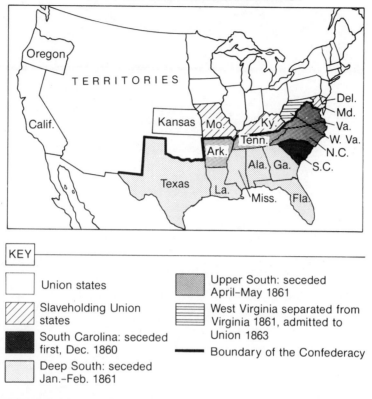

15. Which state seceded first from the Union?

    **(1)** West Virginia
    **(2)** Missouri
    **(3)** South Carolina
    **(4)** Virginia
    **(5)** Georgia

16. Which of the following states was a slaveholding Union state?

    **(1)** Kansas
    **(2)** Kentucky
    **(3)** Texas
    **(4)** Arkansas
    **(5)** California

17. What did Texas do during the Civil War?

    **(1)** It was a Union state that banned slavery.
    **(2)** It remained a slaveholding Union State.
    **(3)** It seceded from the Union in December 1860.
    **(4)** It seceded from the Union in January or February of 1861.
    **(5)** It seceded from the Union in April or May of 1861.

Questions 18–20 are based on the following map.

**TENNESSEE**

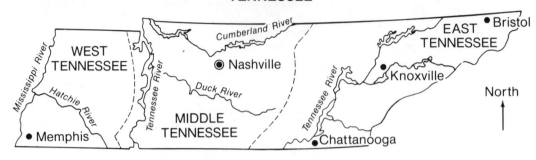

KEY

● Major city
◉ Capital city
--- Regional boundary

18. What major city is located in West Tennessee?

(1) Memphis
(2) Nashville
(3) Bristol
(4) Knoxville
(5) Chattanooga

19. What major city is located on the Tennessee River directly east of the state capital?

(1) Memphis
(2) Nashville
(3) Bristol
(4) Knoxville
(5) Chattanooga

20. What river forms the western border of the state?

(1) the Hatchie River
(2) the Tennessee River
(3) the Duck River
(4) the Cumberland River
(5) the Mississippi River

**Answers start on page 202.**

## CHAPTER REVIEW EVALUATION CHART

| Skill | Question Numbers | Review Pages | Number Correct |
|---|---|---|---|
| Reading a Chart | 1, 2, 3 | 46–51 | _____ /3 |
| Main Idea of a Graph | 6, 10 | 54–59 | _____ /2 |
| Reading a Pictograph | 4, 5 | 60–61 | _____ /2 |
| Reading a Bar Graph | 7 | 62–63 | _____ /1 |
| Reading a Line Graph | 8, 9 | 64–66 | _____ /2 |
| Reading a Circle Graph | 11, 12 | 66–68 | _____ /2 |
| Locating Detail on a Map | 18, 20 | 68–76 | _____ /2 |
| Direction and Distance | 14, 19 | 70–71 | _____ /2 |
| Using a Map Key | 13, 15, 16, 17 | 72–74 | _____ /4 |

Your score: _____ out of 20

Passing score: 15 out of 20

# 3
# Patterns in Social Studies Reading

"Faye, here's the basic cake recipe you wanted. First, cream the butter. Then add the sugar to the butter and mix well. After that, break two eggs and add them to the mixture. Set aside the mixture. Now sift 2 cups flour with ½ teaspoon baking powder and 1 teaspoon salt. Mix the wet ingredients and the dry ingredients and pour the batter into a baking pan. Finally, bake in a 325-degree oven for 45 minutes."

"Why do I need the baking powder, Peg?"

"You need the baking powder to make the cake rise. If you tried to make a cake without baking powder, it would be flat and heavy. Baking powder makes a cake light and fluffy. Even though all the other ingredients are exactly the same, the baking powder makes a big difference."

Peg just showed you some of the ways social studies material is organized. First, when she gave Faye the recipe, she emphasized the **sequence**, or order, of the steps. Then she explained the **effect** of adding the baking powder. Finally, she **compared** and **contrasted** a cake made with baking powder with one made without. In this chapter, we will be looking at these skills:

*Sequence*—getting things in the right order (for example, steps in a recipe)
*Cause and Effect*—understanding what happened and why it happened (for example, the effect of adding ingredients to a recipe)
*Compare and Contrast*—looking at how things and events are the same and how they are different (for example, a cake made with baking powder and a cake made without baking powder)

# SEQUENCE

## Using a Timeline

In this section you will study sequence, the organization of events in time order. Most passages present information in time order. In order to make time sequence clear, you can place events on a timeline. In this book, you will be using timelines that look like this:

earlier

later

The following example shows how to use this kind of timeline.

> The nineteenth century was America's Age of Invention. People like Samuel Morse, Alexander Graham Bell, and Thomas Edison developed devices that changed people's daily lives.
>
> "What hath God wrought?" were the immortal words tapped out by Samuel Morse on his telegraph key in 1837.
>
> "Mr. Watson, come here; I want you," was the first sentence ever spoken on a telephone by its inventor, Alexander Graham Bell, in 1876.
>
> "Mary had a little lamb," were the somewhat less than immortal words recorded by Thomas Edison on his gramophone in 1887.

List the events in the passage you just read on this timeline.

earlier

later

The three events described in the passage are the invention of the telegraph in 1837, the invention of the telephone in 1876, and the invention of the gramophone in 1887.

Your completed timeline should look like this:

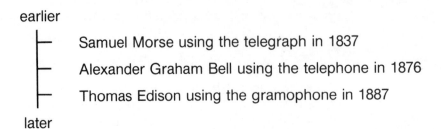

earlier
├─  Samuel Morse using the telegraph in 1837
├─  Alexander Graham Bell using the telephone in 1876
├─  Thomas Edison using the gramophone in 1887
later

---

## Sequence Tip

In addition to dates, words identify sequence. When putting events in time order, look for words like *soon, before, after, later, then,* and *while.*

---

## EXERCISE 1: PUTTING EVENTS IN SEQUENCE

**Passage 1**

*Directions:* Read the following passage. Number the events listed at the end of the passage in the correct order and then write them on the timeline.

> On January 24, 1848, while building a sawmill for John Sutter, James Marshall found some small stones that he thought might contain gold. About a week later, he went to see Sutter at the local fort to show him the stones. Sutter and Marshall tested the stones and found that they were pure gold. Despite their desire to keep their discovery quiet, word spread fast. Soon groups of men were appearing at the mill, looking for gold. Trying to get rid of them, Marshall sent them off in all directions. To his surprise, many of them found gold. The California Gold Rush had begun.

_____ Marshall sends gold seekers off to look for gold.

_____ Marshall and Sutter test the stones to see if they are gold.

_____ Groups of men discover gold in the places where Marshall sent them

_____ Marshall discovers gold at Sutter's mill.

earlier
├─
├─
├─
later

**Passage 2**

*Directions:* Read the following passage. Make a list of the events in the passage. Then construct a timeline like the ones you have been using and put your list of events on it. You should list at least three events on your timeline.

> On October 8, 1871, a cow kicked over a kerosene lamp and started the great Chicago Fire. In a few hours, the fire spread through the West Side and then jumped the South Branch of the Chicago River. The city was in flames.
>
> Twenty-seven hours after it started, the fire was finally put out. Food, clothing, and money began pouring in from all over the world to help the destroyed city.

Your list of events:

Your timeline:

**Answers start on page 203.**

# Sequence Not in Time Order

Passages often present events in an order different from the order in which they occurred. In those cases, you must use clues in the passage to figure out the correct time order. Often you can use dates to help you put events in order, as in the following passage.

> Representing the American colonists, Thomas Jefferson read the Declaration of Independence in Philadelphia on July 4, 1776. The colonists wanted independence from Great Britain because of many conflicts with England.
>
> For example, in 1763, the British had decided that no colonists would be allowed to settle west of the Allegheny Mountains. This angered many colonists who had hoped to move west. Then the Sugar Act of 1764 and the Stamp Act of 1765 forced the colonists to pay heavy taxes to England. Colonists throughout the thirteen colonies opposed these actions. Ten years later, in 1775, the opposition had grown so strong that fighting broke out between the British and the colonists of Massachusetts. It was only a matter of time before the colonies would become an independent nation.

Number the following events in correct time order, using clues from the passage.

_____ Thomas Jefferson reads the Declaration of Independence.

_____ British ban the colonists from moving west of Allegheny Mountains.

_____ Fighting breaks out between the British and the colonists of Massachusetts.

_____ The British force the colonists to pay heavy taxes.

Now place the events in order on the timeline.

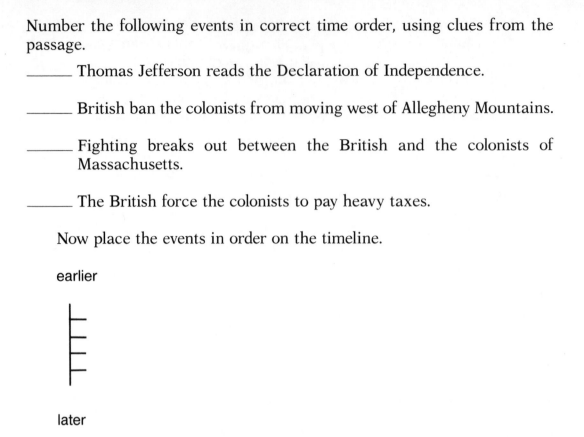

earlier

later

In this passage, the writer presents events out of time order in order to emphasize the main point. The main idea, that the Declaration of Independence was the result of a long series of conflicts, is made in the first sentence. The description of events in the second paragraph supports that main idea. Even though the reading of the Declaration of Independence happened after the other events, the author mentions it first in order to make his main idea clear. Your completed timeline should look like this:

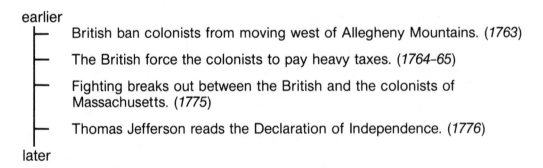

earlier

— British ban colonists from moving west of Allegheny Mountains. (*1763*)

— The British force the colonists to pay heavy taxes. (*1764–65*)

— Fighting breaks out between the British and the colonists of Massachusetts. (*1775*)

— Thomas Jefferson reads the Declaration of Independence. (*1776*)

later

## EXERCISE 2: USING DATES TO IDENTIFY SEQUENCE

*Directions:* Following the passage on page 91 is a list of the events described in the passage. Number the events, fill in their dates, and place them in correct order on the timeline.

Following the European discovery of America by Christopher Columbus in 1492, other nations sent explorers and settlers to North America. The Spanish were ruthless and bloodthirsty. One Spanish explorer, Hernando De Soto, marched through the southeastern United States from 1539 to 1542. He used torture to force the Indians to lead him to gold. Since there was almost no gold to be found, he killed many Indians. The worst massacre occurred at the Indian settlement of Mabila on the Alabama River, where De Soto's men murdered several thousand Indians.

The French also sent explorers to North America, but they treated the Indians well and traded with them. When Jacques Cartier discovered the mouth of the St. Lawrence River in 1534, he opened up Canada to French exploration. From 1603 to 1615, Samuel de Champlain explored parts of southern Canada and northern New York and established the fur trade with the Indians. Over fifty years later, Marquette and Joliet traveled down the Mississippi River as far as Arkansas, establishing French claims to the entire Mississippi valley.

_____ Columbus discovers America.
        date: _____

_____ De Soto murders thousands of Indians at Mabila.
        approximate date: _____

_____ Cartier discovers the mouth of the St. Lawrence River.
        date: _____

_____ Marquette and Joliet travel down the Mississippi River.
        approximate date: _____

_____ Champlain establishes the fur trade with the Indians.
        approximate date: _____

earlier

later

**Answers start on page 203.**

# Sequence in Graphs

A line graph is well suited to showing a trend over time. By showing how something changes over time, a graph illustrates a sequence very clearly. The following line graph traces the price of chicken at Piggle-Wiggle Supermarkets from 1980 to 1987. Answer the question following the graph by circling the correct choice.

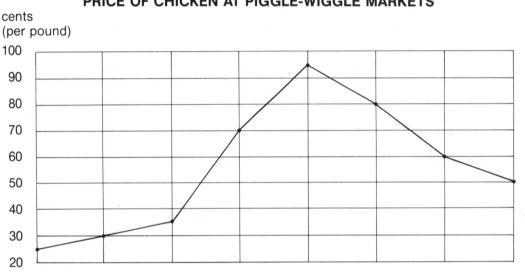

**PRICE OF CHICKEN AT PIGGLE-WIGGLE MARKETS**

Between 1980 and 1984, the price of chicken at Piggle-Wiggle Markets

- **(1)** went down
- **(2)** went up
- **(3)** went down and then up
- **(4)** went up and then down
- **(5)** remained steady

You were correct if you circled choice (2). Find the data points for 1980 and 1984. Now look at the part of the line between them. The line goes up at each point. This means that the price of chicken went up from 1980 to 1984.

## EXERCISE 3: SEQUENCE IN GRAPHS

*Directions:* Study the following graph, then choose the number of the correct answer to each question.

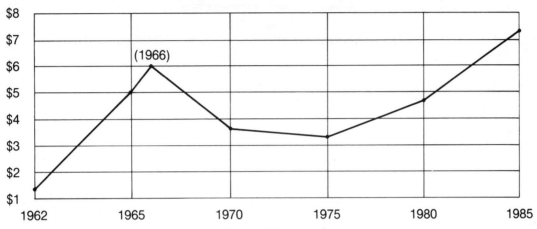

**HOW MUCH NASA SPENT**
**In Billions of Dollars Per Year**

Source: Office of Management and Budget/*Chicago Tribune*

**1.** Between 1965 and 1970, NASA spending

   **(1)** rose and then fell
   **(2)** dropped steadily
   **(3)** rose slightly
   **(4)** remained constant
   **(5)** dropped and then rose

**2.** Between 1975 and 1985, NASA spending

   **(1)** decreased
   **(2)** increased
   **(3)** increased then decreased
   **(4)** decreased then increased
   **(5)** remained level

**3.** Which of the following best describes the pattern of NASA spending between 1962 and 1985?

   **(1)** It rose steadily.
   **(2)** It rose, then fell.
   **(3)** It peaked in 1975.
   **(4)** It rose until 1966, fell until 1980, then rose again.
   **(5)** It rose until 1966, fell until 1975, then rose again.

**Answers start on page 203.**

# Sequence on Expedition Maps

Maps can depict a chain of events or changes over time. For example, the route of an explorer or an army could be traced on a map. Study the following example to see how looking at the route of the explorers Lewis and Clark can help us understand their journey.

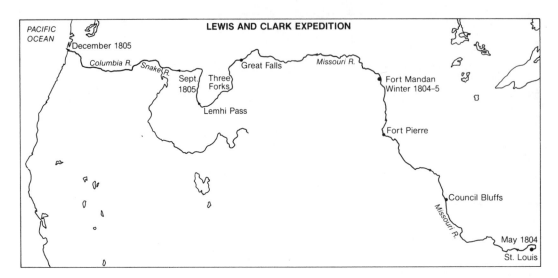

▶ When did Lewis and Clark leave St. Louis? _____

In order to find when Lewis and Clark left St. Louis, you must find St. Louis on the map. If you are not sure where St. Louis is, trace along the line that represents the route of Lewis and Clark until you find St. Louis. It is at the eastern end of their route. The date May 1804 is written next to the city. That is the date that Lewis and Clark left St. Louis.

▶ Where did Lewis and Clark spend the winter of 1804–5?

_____

Trace the route of the expedition until you find the Winter 1804–05. Winter 1804–05 is written above Fort Mandan. Therefore, they spent the winter at Fort Mandan.

▶ When did Lewis and Clark reach the Pacific Ocean? _____

Trace the route of the expedition until it reaches the Pacific Ocean. You should find the date December 1805, which is the date the expedition reached the Pacific Ocean.

## EXERCISE 4: EXPEDITION MAPS

*Directions:* Answer each question by circling the number of the correct choice. This map shows the route of a famous explorer through what is now the southeastern United States.

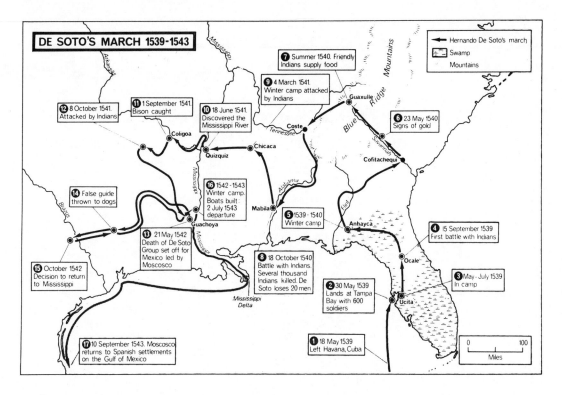

1. Where did De Soto first enter what is now the United States?

   **(1)** Havana, Cuba
   **(2)** Mississippi Delta
   **(3)** Brazos River
   **(4)** Tampa Bay
   **(5)** Guachoya

2. Where did friendly Indians supply food to De Soto?

   **(1)** Tampa Bay
   **(2)** Quizquiz
   **(3)** Guaxulle
   **(4)** Mabila
   **(5)** Ocale

3. When did De Soto die?

   **(1)** September 1539
   **(2)** October 1540
   **(3)** June 1541
   **(4)** May 1542
   **(5)** September 1543

**4.** What important event happened at Quizquiz?

   **(1)** Several thousand Indians were killed.
   **(2)** De Soto died.
   **(3)** Friendly Indians supplied food.
   **(4)** A bison was caught.
   **(5)** The Mississippi River was discovered.

**Answers start on page 203.**

# Sequence on Maps of Historical Change

    Maps can illustrate a trend over time of either growth or decline of an area. The varying boundaries of nations, areas of settlement, or areas of production of a product can all be depicted on maps. The map below shows the pattern of settlement of the thirteen original U.S. colonies over time.

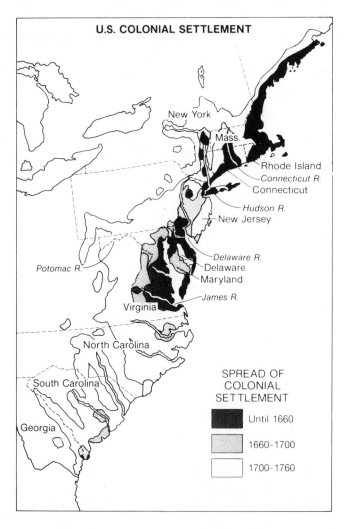

▶ Until 1660, most of the settlement was along the coast of the Atlantic Ocean. True or False? _____

You were right if you thought the statement was true. Find the areas that match the key for the areas settled before 1660. These areas are mainly along the coast, as well as along the James, Hudson, and Connecticut rivers.

▶ In general, most of the early colonists settled south of Virginia, with settlement spreading north in later years. True or False? _____

You were right if you thought the statement was false. Just the opposite is true. The early settlement was in the northern part of the country from Maine to Virginia. Settlement then spread south through the Carolinas and Georgia.

▶ With the passage of time, settlement spread inland from the coast. True or False? _____

You were right if you thought the statement was true. The area for 1660-1700 and the area for 1700-1760 show a steady growth inland.

## EXERCISE 5: READING MAPS OF HISTORICAL CHANGE

*Directions:* Mark each statement true (T) or false (F) based on the map. This map shows how the United States expanded into its current 48 continental states.

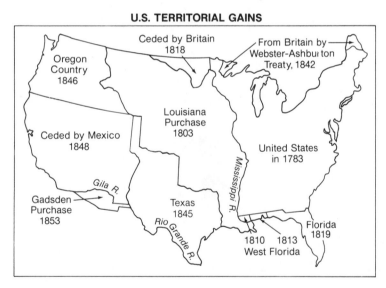

**U.S. TERRITORIAL GAINS**

_____ **1.** The Southwest was ceded by Mexico after the Oregon Country was already under United States control.

_____ **2.** The Louisiana Purchase was the first major territorial gain for the United States after 1783.

_____ **3.** After the Mexican cession in 1848, the United States controlled all the land that would become the continental 48 states.

_____ **4.** Florida was completely under the control of the United States by 1813.

**Answers start on page 204.**

# UNDERSTANDING CAUSE AND EFFECT

## Identifying Cause and Effect

Every day you are affected by what goes on around you. In order to function in your daily life, you have to understand cause and effect. For example, if you didn't pay your rent every month, you would be evicted from your home. The cause would be not paying the rent. The effect would be eviction.

*cause:*                                 *effect:*

not paying rent ————————➤ eviction

Sometimes cause and effect can be very clear. A sixteen-year-old student cuts school sixty-eight days. The effect is that she is not promoted. At other times, cause-and-effect relationships are less clear. "I wish I knew what I could have done to help him stop drinking." Much of political debate is about causes and effects. One politician says, "If we raise taxes, the economy will improve." At the same time, another says, "If we lower taxes, the economy will improve."

When reading social studies passages, you should ask yourself "What happened?" and "Why did it happen?" When you answer the question "What happened?" you understand the *effect*. When you answer the question "Why did it happen?" you understand the *cause*. Your reading will often contain clues that can help you decide what is the cause and what is the effect.

Read the following sentence. Decide what happened and why it happened and fill in the blanks.

Because it was mismanaged, the company went bankrupt.

▶ What happened? _____

▶ Why did it happen? _____

You should have written "The company went bankrupt" as the answer to the first question and "Because it was mismanaged" as the answer to the second. *Because* is a clue word for the *cause* or the answer to "Why did it happen?"

---

### Cause and Effect Tip

Watch for cause-and-effect clue words and phrases in your reading like *because* and *as a result of. Before* and *after* sometimes also function as cause-and-effect clue words.

## EXERCISE 6: IDENTIFYING CAUSE AND EFFECT

*Directions:* For each sentence, decide what happened (the effect) and why it happened (the cause) and then fill in the blanks with your choices.

**1.** Because the wholesale price of coffee had dropped 25%, Colombia found itself in financial trouble.

What happened? _____

Why did it happen? _____

**2.** The American West developed rapidly after the Civil War because of the railroads.

What happened? _____

Why did it happen? _____

**3.** Oil prices increased dramatically as a result of the formation of the oil cartel OPEC in 1973.

What happened? _____

Why did it happen? _____

**4.** After man-made rubber was developed, the price of natural rubber dropped.

What happened? _____

Why did it happen? _____

**Answers start on page 204.**

# Identifying Cause and Effect in a Passage

You cannot depend on a cause and effect always being in the same sentence or being clearly pointed out. You should remember to ask the key questions: "What happened?" (effect) and "Why did it happen?" (cause). In the paragraph below, underline the cause and circle the effect.

> Mothers Against Drunk Drivers (MADD), Students Against Drunk Drivers (SADD), and Bartenders Against Drunk Drivers (BADD) have all campaigned against driving while drinking. The result has been a decrease in traffic accidents.

The key word *result* can help you find what happened (the effect): a decrease in traffic accidents. The first sentence explains why it happened (the cause): MADD, SADD, and BADD all campaigned against drunk driving.

## EXERCISE 7: CAUSE AND EFFECT IN A PASSAGE

*Directions:* Following each passage are questions about cause and effect. Circle the number of the correct choice.

Our continent is named for one of the greatest frauds of all time, Amerigo Vespucci. Vespucci helped outfit Columbus's fleet for his third voyage in 1498. During that voyage, Columbus first sighted the mainland of America. In order to beat Columbus's claim, Vespucci published an account of a voyage he had headed in 1497. This voyage never took place.

After reading Vespucci's false account, the king of Portugal asked him to accompany the Portuguese explorer Coelho and write about the voyage. Vespucci went on two voyages commanded by Coelho. In his writings, he took full credit for both voyages and never mentioned Coelho.

Vespucci's accounts were read by many people because he included stories of native sexual customs. In 1507, a young professor of geography in France placed the name *America* on what we now call *South America*. The name caught on. By the time people agreed that Columbus had really discovered the New World, it was too late. The name *America* had been given to the entire New World.

1. What was the effect of Vespucci's false account of his voyage to the new world in 1497?

   **(1)** Vespucci became the first explorer to discover America.
   **(2)** The King of Portugal forced Vespucci to leave Portugal.
   **(3)** The King of Portugal asked Vespucci to accompany Coelho.
   **(4)** Coelho gave Vespucci credit for Coelho's expeditions.
   **(5)** Coelho came to value Vespucci's great knowledge of America.

2. What caused Vespucci's accounts of his voyages with Coelho to be read by so many people?

   **(1)** He wrote about native sexual customs.
   **(2)** Vespucci made Coelho famous.
   **(3)** The whole world focused on the daring Portuguese explorers.
   **(4)** A French geography professor had all his students study Vespucci's work.
   **(5)** Vespucci was the famous discoverer of America.

In December 1984, a deadly gas leak from a Union Carbide plant in Bhopal, India, killed 1,700 people and injured another 200,000. Although Union Carbide is an American company, lawsuits resulting from the accident are being handled by Indian courts. A U.S. District Court judge ruled that the lawsuits should be heard in India because the witnesses and evidence are there.

Damage awards in Indian courts tend to be much lower than awards in U.S. courts. As a result, victims of the accident will probably receive less money than they would if their cases were handled in the U.S.

**3.** A U.S. District Court judge ruled that the Bhopal cases should be handled in India because

**(1)** damage awards are generally lower in India
**(2)** Union Carbide is an American company
**(3)** accident victims don't need large damage awards
**(4)** Indian courts aren't as busy as U.S. courts
**(5)** the witnesses and evidence are in India

**4.** Victims will probably receive smaller awards than they would if their cases were handled in the U.S. because

**(1)** 1,700 people were killed and over 200,000 people injured
**(2)** the witnesses and evidence are in India
**(3)** judges in the U.S. take these claims less seriously
**(4)** damage awards in Indian courts tend to be lower
**(5)** Union Carbide is an American company

In the 1920s, psychologists Hugh Hartshorne and Mark A. May studied the development of honesty by testing 11,000 children. As a result of the tests, they decided that the children did not develop honesty as a result of preaching by adults. Instead, they learned honesty mainly through personal relationships and social situations.

Hartshorne and May saw the children imitating adult and peer models a great deal. In other words, they found that the children did what they saw others do, not what they were told to do. If the children were surrounded by lying, cheating, and stealing, they tended to lie, cheat, and steal. If the people they imitated were honest, they tended to be honest.

**5.** According to Hartshorne and May, children are likely to be honest if

**(1)** they are often in social situations
**(2)** the people around them are honest
**(3)** they are told they should be honest
**(4)** their families have plenty of money
**(5)** they are punished for dishonesty

**Answers start on page 204.**

# Applying Cause and Effect

Government has a strong effect on our lives as Americans. American blacks are one group whose lives have been affected, for good or bad, by the actions of the government. In the next exercise, you will be asked to match four actions of government with the effect each action might have had on an individual person.

## EXERCISE 8: APPLYING CAUSE AND EFFECT

*Directions:* Below are listed four documents that greatly influenced conditions for black Americans. Below the documents are quotes that describe the effect of each of these documents. Match each government action with the quote it made possible.

**a.** Emancipation Proclamation—1863
President Lincoln ordered an end to slavery in the Confederate states.

**b.** Supreme Court separate-but-equal decision—1896
Segregation of public facilities such as schools was declared legal by the Supreme Court.

**c.** Voting Rights Act—1965
Laws preventing black people from voting were banned by Congress.

**d.** Civil Rights Act—1964
Discrimination in public places was banned by Congress.

_____ **1.** "As our first black mayor, I pledge to serve all the people."

_____ **2.** "I remember when I had to sit in the back of the bus. Now I can sit where I please."

_____ **3.** "I have to go to a separate school from white people. Some people say they are just as good, but I don't believe them."

_____ **4.** "I'm a free man now. I'm going to join the Union army and fight the slaveholders."

**Answers start on page 204.**

# COMPARISON AND CONTRAST

## Looking at Similarities

Despite the great differences among human societies, anthropologists have found an institution they all share. All societies have some form of marriage.

The above paragraph compares the societies of the world. It looks for similarities shared by all and finds one: marriage. A **comparison** can show how two or more things are alike. Read the following paragraph. Then, in the blank provided, write one way that the Coney Island amusement parks were similar.

New York's Coney Island amusement parks were all designed to send people into a world of pleasure. For instance, Steeplechase Park was nicknamed "The Funny Place." It featured rides such as the human roulette wheel, which sent riders whirling and sprawling. Its "Blowhole Theatre" contained hidden air jets that blew off men's hats and sent ladies' skirts flying up around their waists. Luna Park was a dream city of bright colors and fanciful decorations. It was exotic, rich, and magical. Visitors felt as though they had entered a foreign land when they walked through the gates of Luna Park.

▶ How were all the amusement parks similar?

_____

The first sentence tells you that all the parks were designed to send people into a world of pleasure. The clue word *all* tells you that a similarity is being described.

## EXERCISE 9: IDENTIFYING SIMILARITIES

*Directions:* In your own words, answer the questions following each passage.

> The populations of three major races, the Caucasians, the Negroes, and the Mongolians, all developed in a similar way. Large numbers of each race abandoned hunting and gathering and turned to agriculture. The result in each case was population growth among the agricultural groups. Those groups that remained hunters and gatherers, such as the Pygmies and Bushmen of Africa and the aborigines of Australia, now make up only a tiny percentage of the world population.

**1.** Why did the three major races all experience population growth?

_____

**2.** How are the Pygmies and Bushmen of Africa and the aborigines of Australia similar?

_____

> The two nations of Great Britain and Japan have much in common. Both are large island nations separated from the mainland by narrow bodies of water. Both were once major military powers controlling vast amounts of land and millions of people. While neither is important today for its military might, both Great Britain and Japan are important industrial and trading nations.

**3.** How is the geography of Great Britain and Japan similar?

_____

**4.** How is the history of Japan and Great Britain similar?

_____

**5.** How are the economies of Great Britain and Japan similar today?

_____

**Possible answers start on page 204.**

# Looking at Differences

You have looked at similarities. Now you will look at differences. When you **contrast** two things, you concentrate on how they are different. Examining differences as well as similarities helps you get a better picture of what you are studying. Read the following example passage, then use the information in the passage to fill in the chart.

In the past 200 years, technology has changed our lives radically. For example, while our ancestors depended on horses to travel long distances, today we travel from coast to coast in a few hours on an airplane. When we want to get around town, we may drive a car, or we may take a high-speed subway train.

Another dramatic change we have experienced has been in communication. The Battle of New Orleans was fought because neither side knew that the War of 1812 had already ended. It took weeks for the news to travel by boat from England to the United States. Today, through radio and television, we have almost instant access to world events. In addition, world leaders can talk on the telephone even though they may be separated by an ocean.

Now use the information in the passage above to fill in this chart. In your own words, write information in each box that contrasts travel and communication today and 200 years ago.

| CONTRAST: 200 YEARS AGO AND TODAY | | |
|---|---|---|
| | **200 Years Ago** | **Today** |
| travel | | |
| overseas communication | | |

Your chart might look something like this. Did you show how different things are now than they were 200 years ago?

| CONTRAST: 200 YEARS AGO AND TODAY | | |
|---|---|---|
| | **200 Years Ago** | **Today** |
| travel | depended on horses so long-distance travel very slow | can get around town or even coast to coast very fast |
| overseas communication | messages had to travel by boat across the ocean | now can talk on the phone overseas; hear radio and TV news the same day something happens |

## EXERCISE 10: IDENTIFYING CONTRASTS

*Directions:* Read the following passage. Then fill in the chart to show how the Uptown Jews and the Downtown Jews were different.

By the late 1800s, New York City was home for two very different groups of Jewish immigrants: the Uptown Jews and the Downtown Jews. Many of the Uptown Jews were of German descent, but they had been born in America. Many of them settled in the wealthy Upper East Side and Upper West Side neighborhoods of New York City. They were Reform Jews, so they did not *keep kosher* (follow Jewish dietary laws).

These Uptown Jews differed in many ways from the Jews who were joining them in New York City. The Downtown Jews came to this country from Eastern Europe in the late 1800s. Most of them had very little money. They moved into the poorer Lower East Side neighborhoods. As Orthodox Jews, they followed more traditional Jewish practices than the Uptown Jews and continued to keep kosher.

|  | Uptown Jews | Downtown Jews |
|---|---|---|
| where were they born? |  |  |
| where did they live in New York City? |  |  |
| did they keep kosher? |  |  |
| were they wealthy? |  |  |

**Answers start on page 205.**

# Comparison and Contrast in Illustrations

Maps, charts, and graphs can be used to illustrate comparison and contrast. For example, the map on page 107 compares and contrasts black voting rights in Southern states during the early years of the civil rights movement. Answer the questions based on the map.

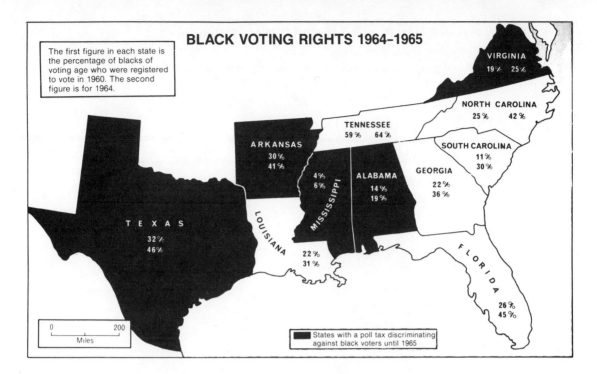

**BLACK VOTING RIGHTS 1964–1965**

The first figure in each state is the percentage of blacks of voting age who were registered to vote in 1960. The second figure is for 1964.

VIRGINIA 19% 25%

NORTH CAROLINA 25% 42%

TENNESSEE 59% 64%

ARKANSAS 30% 41%

SOUTH CAROLINA 11% 30%

GEORGIA 22% 36%

ALABAMA 14% 19%

MISSISSIPPI 4% 6%

TEXAS 32% 46%

LOUISIANA 22% 31%

FLORIDA 26% 45%

0    200
Miles

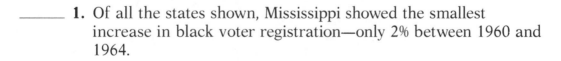

States with a poll tax discriminating against black voters until 1965

▶ Which five states used a poll tax to discriminate against blacks until 1965? _____

You were right if you listed Texas, Arkansas, Mississippi, Alabama, and Virginia. These states are all shaded black on the map, showing that they used a poll tax.

▶ Between 1960 and 1964, did North Carolina or South Carolina have a greater increase in the percentage of registered black voters? _____

You were right if you said South Carolina had a greater increase, from 11% to 30%, or an increase of 19%. North Carolina increased from 25% to 42%, or an increase of 17%.

## EXERCISE 11: COMPARISON AND CONTRAST IN ILLUSTRATIONS

*Directions:* Mark each statement *T* if it is true or *F* if it is false.
Questions 1–2 are based on the map "Black Voting Rights" above.

_____ **1.** Of all the states shown, Mississippi showed the smallest increase in black voter registration—only 2% between 1960 and 1964.

_____ **2.** In 1964, Texas had the highest percentage of any southern state of eligible blacks registered, with 46%.

Questions 3–6 are based on the following line graph.

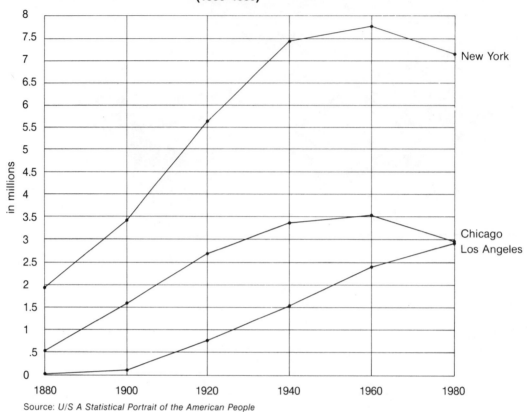

**THE THREE LARGEST CITIES IN 1980 AND
THEIR POPULATIONS IN EARLIER YEARS
(1880–1980)**

Source: *U/S A Statistical Portrait of the American People*

_____ **3.** When the population of New York City was increasing, the population of Chicago was also increasing.

_____ **4.** New York and Chicago have always had about the same population.

_____ **5.** In 1980, Chicago and Los Angeles had about the same population.

_____ **6.** When the population of Chicago was decreasing, the population of Los Angeles was also decreasing.

**Answers start on page 205.**

## EXERCISE 12: CHAPTER REVIEW

*Directions:* Study each passage or illustration carefully. Then choose the correct answer to each question.

Questions 1–3 are based on the following map.

**SPREAD OF THE COTTON KINGDOM**

1. In 1801, the Cotton Kingdom was centered in

   (1) Texas, Indian Territory, and Arkansas
   (2) the Carolinas, Georgia, and Virginia
   (3) Georgia, Alabama, Mississippi, Louisiana
   (4) Florida and Texas
   (5) Tennessee, Alabama, and Mississippi

2. From 1801 to 1860, the spread of the Cotton Kingdom was to

   (1) the north and east
   (2) the south and west
   (3) the east
   (4) Illinois
   (5) the Atlantic coast

3. The areas that had the greatest growth from 1801 to 1839 in land devoted to cotton were

   (1) Texas, Indian Territory, and Arkansas
   (2) the Carolinas, Georgia, and Virginia
   (3) Georgia, Alabama, Mississippi, Louisiana
   (4) Florida and Texas
   (5) Tennessee, Kentucky, and North Carolina

Questions 4–5 are based on the following passage.

The epidemic of adolescent drug abuse continues to rage across the nation. Many reasons are given to explain this problem. Some people say that parents are too easy on their children. Other people say that the problem is caused by people drifting away from religion. Probably one of the main causes of the problem is peer pressure—teenagers just want to be part of the gang. Another reason kids take drugs is the desire to escape reality. Drugs seem to provide a way out from the pressures of growing up. Drugs also seem glamorous because they are forbidden.

The effects of drug abuse can be devastating. A drug abuser might radically change in both appearance and behavior. The desperate need for money to buy drugs can lead the user to prostitution or robbery. In addition, adolescent drug abuse places a terrible strain on family relationships.

4. According to the passage, one of the main causes of adolescent drug abuse is probably

    (1) peer pressure
    (2) strained family relationships
    (3) a radical change in appearance and behavior
    (4) a desperate need for money
    (5) teen prostitution

5. According to the passage, drug abuse may cause an adolescent to

    (1) drift away from religion
    (2) commit crimes
    (3) want to be part of the gang
    (4) become more loving toward his or her family
    (5) improve his or her appearance

Questions 6–10 are based on the following passage.

When high-tech industries are struggling, the next high-tech boom may be getting started. When laid-off executives and scientists don't have enough to do, they dream of running their own companies or building new products. So they start new companies offering new products.

Thus, while the giant companies suffer through hard times, dozens of new companies are quietly setting up shop. Often these new firms create the new products of the next boom. When these breakthrough products capture the public's imagination, the new boom explodes. Old and new firms rush to copy the product. The industry shoots into a period of frantic growth that may last two years or more.

Then the public's love affair with the product ends. Or a
giant company takes over the whole market. Then the boom is
over. The industry slumps back into the next recession. This
bust-boom-bust cycle has happened over and over in high
technology: in the late 1960s with minicomputers, in the mid-70s
with personal computers and video games, and in the early '80s
with personal computer peripherals, VCRs, and software.

6. How were the high-tech booms of the late 1960s, the mid-1970s, and
the early 1980s similar?

**(1)** They all got started when new firms introduced new products.
**(2)** They were all related to the car industry.
**(3)** They all ended when one giant company took over the market.
**(4)** They all began during times of prosperity.
**(5)** They were all dominated by the Japanese.

7. How were the high-tech booms of the late 1960s, the mid-1970s and
the early '80s different?

**(1)** Their patterns of boom and decline are different.
**(2)** Only in the mid-70s did firms rush to copy the new product.
**(3)** Only in the early '80s was there a major new breakthrough
product.
**(4)** Different products led each boom.
**(5)** Economic conditions were very different while the new products
and new companies were getting started.

8. What is the correct sequence of each high-tech boom cycle?

**(1)** large companies develop new product, new market booms,
industry slumps
**(2)** development during previous boom, short recession, new boom
**(3)** development of new product by new firm during slow period,
boom, industry slump
**(4)** company mergers, development of new product, booming new
market, leveling off
**(5)** mass advertising campaign, booming sales, new firms created,
period of stability

9. What is one of the causes of a high-tech boom?

**(1)** planning by giant corporations during times of prosperity
**(2)** government regulation that directs the industry in the most
productive direction
**(3)** executives and scientists developing firms and products during a
slow period
**(4)** a giant competitor dominating the market
**(5)** market surveys that indicate the area of greatest consumer need

**10.** According to the passage, which of the following might cause a high-tech boom to end?

   **(1)** scientists developing a new product
   **(2)** the public losing interest in the new product
   **(3)** other firms copying the product
   **(4)** computers becoming obsolete
   **(5)** executives getting laid off

**Answers start on page 205.**

## CHAPTER REVIEW EVALUATION CHART

| Reading Skill | Question Numbers* | Review Pages | Number Correct |
|---|---|---|---|
| Sequence | **1, 2, 3**, 8 | 86–97 | _____ /4 |
| Cause-Effect | 4, 5, 9, 10 | 98–102 | _____ /4 |
| Compare-Contrast | 6, 7 | 103–108 | _____ /2 |

*Question numbers in **dark type** are based on illustrations.

Your score: _____ out of 10

Passing score: 7 out of 10

# 4
# Analyzing Social Studies Passages

Eileen's eighteen-year-old son Greg just got his driver's license. As Eileen walked into the house with two bags of groceries, Greg rushed to her side, took the bags from her, and put away the groceries. When he finished, Eileen said, "OK, you can have the car tonight."

Eileen was using her analytical skills. She looked at the facts: Greg had never helped her with the groceries before. Greg had just gotten his driver's license.

She realized that he must be helping her in order to get something else. He must want to use the car. Greg also was using his analytical skills. He predicted that if he helped his mother she might let him use her car.

In this chapter, you will be practicing these analytical skills:

**1.** Distinguishing fact from opinion

fact: Greg is helping with the groceries.
opinion: Greg is a good son.

**2.** Making inferences, or reading between the lines

Greg helps me only when he wants something. He is helping me now. Therefore, he must want something.

**3.** Developing a hypothesis, or educated guess

Since Greg just got his license, a reasonable explanation of why he is helping is that he wants to use the car.

**4.** Predicting an outcome

Mom will let me use the car if I help her with the groceries.

You will also begin to study political cartoons and how they use comedy and exaggeration to express opinions.

# FACT AND OPINION

## Distinguishing Fact from Opinion

A *fact* is a statement that can be proven. An *opinion* is a belief that cannot be proven. If someone believes that something is true, it still has to be proven to be a fact. Every day, you read and hear both facts and opinions. At times, you may have to give some thought to which is which. When you read social studies material, take note of whether a statement you read is fact or opinion. Can a statement be proven? Or is it something the author believes but cannot prove?

Of the following two statements, one is a fact and one is an opinion. Write *F* in the blank before the fact and *O* in the blank before the opinion.

_____ The U.S. Constitution is the greatest political document ever written.

_____ In 1985, there were twenty-six amendments to the U.S. Constitution.

You were right if you thought the first statement was an opinion. The word *greatest* gives the opinion of the writer. The second statement is a fact that can be checked by looking at a copy of the Constitution.

### EXERCISE 1: FACT OR OPINION?

*Directions:* In the blank preceding each sentence, write *F* if the sentence is a fact and *O* if it is an opinion.

**1.** _____ The United States is a democracy in which people elect their government officials.

**2.** _____ Democracy is the best form of government.

**3.** _____ Local governments mismanage their responsibilities of police and fire protection.

**4.** _____ Local governments have responsibility for the public schools.

**5.** _____ All citizens over the age of eighteen have the right to register and vote.

**6.** _____ The vice president has the most unimportant job in the entire federal government.

**7.** _____ If the president dies in office, the vice president becomes the new president.

**Answers start on page 205.**

# Facts and Opinions in a Passage

Writers often tell you facts and express their opinions in the same piece of writing. They use the facts as evidence to back up their opinions. In the following example, see how the author uses facts to support her opinion. Read the paragraph and underline the sentences that contain facts. Circle the sentences that contain opinions.

> The United States is a member of the North Atlantic Treaty Organization (NATO). The members of NATO coordinate their military activity in Europe through the NATO military command. Because we have to work through the NATO chain of command, NATO restricts our ability to act on our own. We should withdraw from NATO because our military needs to be able to work freely in Europe.

The first two sentences are facts. The writer can prove that the United States is a member of NATO. She can also prove that NATO has a military command that coordinates the activity of member nations in Europe. The second two sentences are opinions. It is her opinion that membership in NATO restricts our ability to act on our own. In the last sentence, the word _should_ is a clue that the sentence is the opinion of the author. She is telling you what she thinks _should_ happen.

---

### Fact vs. Opinion Tip

Phrases like _I think, I believe,_ and _we should_ tell you that an opinion is being expressed.

## EXERCISE 2: FACTS AND OPINIONS IN A PASSAGE

*Directions:* For each sentence in each of the following passages, write *F* if the sentence is a fact and *O* if the sentence is an opinion.

### Passage 1

**(a)** The best political system ever developed is the two-party system of the United States. **(b)** Since the Civil War, no third party has been able to threaten the political power of either the Democratic Party or the Republican Party. **(c)** Every president of the last one hundred years has been a member of one of these two parties. **(d)** No third party has been able to gain control of either house of Congress. **(e)** The country has been spared the chaos that results when there are more than two parties. **(f)** And the people have not had to endure the tyranny of one-party rule.

a. _____     d. _____

b. _____     e. _____

c. _____     f. _____

### Passage 2

**(a)** The book *The Hard Times of Mortimer Mitchell* should not be on the shelves of our high school library. **(b)** First, the characters take drugs. **(c)** Second, there are three scenes in the book in which sexual activity between unmarried people is described in detail. **(d)** Third, the main character murders another character and then goes unpunished. **(e)** This is not the kind of book that the children in our community should read. **(f)** A parent committee should be formed to help the school librarian choose good reading material for our teens.

a. _____     d. _____

b. _____     e. _____

c. _____     f. _____

**Answers start on page 205.**

# READING BETWEEN THE LINES

## Making an Inference

The information in a passage is not always stated directly. A writer will often provide clues to facts or to his opinions and then leave it up to you to figure them out. Figuring out unstated facts and opinions is often called *reading between the lines* or *making an inference*.

## Inferring Facts

A passage can suggest a fact by giving you clues that you can gather as you read. As you read the following paragraph, watch for clues to Tanya and Mira's ages and their relationship. What is the writer telling you that he is not stating directly?

> Mira and Tanya couldn't decide what television program to watch. There were many different cartoon shows on Saturday morning, and they liked them all. They didn't want to help their father make breakfast. So they decided to ride their bikes.

▶ In what age group are Tanya and Mira?

**(1)** babies
**(2)** children
**(3)** teenagers
**(4)** young adults
**(5)** senior citizens

clues: _____

You were right if you chose (2). There are several clues that Tanya and Mira are children. They were interested in Saturday morning cartoons. They went outside to ride their bikes. These are activities that children enjoy.

▶ What is the relationship between Tanya and Mira?

**(1)** sisters
**(2)** friends
**(3)** parent-child
**(4)** co-workers
**(5)** boyfriend-girlfriend

clue: _____

You were right if you chose (1). The third sentence tells you their father is making breakfast.

## EXERCISE 3: INFERRING FACTS
### Part A
*Directions:* Following this passage are two inferences that can be drawn from the passage. List at least one clue for each inference.

> I had worked hard all day and was very tired. This white
> man walked back, expecting me to get up and give him my seat.
> I refused. In most parts of the world, a man would give up his
> seat to a woman, but I was arrested for refusing to move for the
> white man. The black community rallied to my support,
> beginning the famous Montgomery, Alabama, bus boycott.

**1.** Inference: The incident described in the passage occurred on a bus.

   clues: _____

**2.** Inference: The speaker in the passage is a black woman.

   clues: _____

### Part B
*Directions:* Read the following passages and answer the questions. The correct answers to the questions are not stated directly in the passages, but they can be inferred. Be sure you have found at least one clue that backs up the answer you choose.

> Sam's life was very hard. He was expected to be out
> working in the cotton fields by sunrise. No matter how hot it
> was, the foreman kept him working until sunset. His owner had
> paid $25 for him and expected to get his money's worth.

**1.** Sam was

   **(1)** a migrant farm worker
   **(2)** a slave
   **(3)** a technician
   **(4)** the owner of a small farm
   **(5)** a foreman

> Two hundred of us were working on the floor when the fire
> broke out. Rolls of fabric were piled everywhere. There was
> barely enough room to walk between the sewing machines.
> Some of the other women I work with began to panic when they
> discovered that the fire escape door was locked. Somehow I
> managed to get down the stairway and down to the street. I saw
> women leaping from the windows. It seemed that dead bodies
> were everywhere.

**2.** The speaker in the passage was

   **(1)** an owner of a large mill
   **(2)** a New England farmer
   **(3)** an immigrant awaiting entry to the United States
   **(4)** a worker at a factory
   **(5)** a newspaper reporter writing about a fire

**3.** Where does this passage take place?

   **(1)** a farm
   **(2)** a one-story mill
   **(3)** a residential neighborhood
   **(4)** a fire station
   **(5)** a multistory factory

> When I took office, the country was in the middle of the worst economic period of its history. Unemployment was very high and many farms and businesses had gone bankrupt. I felt that government should take a more active role in helping people. I proposed programs to Congress to restore people's hope in the future. In a few years, bank accounts were insured by the government, the Tennessee Valley Authority was generating low-cost power, farmers had some protection, and unemployed workers could labor on public works projects. But, despite all my efforts, hard times continued for some years.

**4.** The person speaking in this paragraph is

   **(1)** Douglas MacArthur, a general in the United States Army
   **(2)** Woody Guthrie, a songwriter who wrote of people's hardships
   **(3)** Franklin D. Roosevelt, president of the United States from 1933 to 1945
   **(4)** Samuel Gompers, president of the American Federation of Labor from 1886 to 1924
   **(5)** Andrew Carnegie, one of the men who built American industry in the 1800s

**Answers start on page 206.**

# Inferring Opinions

You have been learning to infer facts that are not stated directly in a passage. Authors often also imply opinions in their writing. You can infer opinions in the same way as facts—by looking at the evidence. When you are figuring out opinions that are not stated directly, be careful with the evidence. It is very easy to substitute your own ideas for the ideas of the writer if you don't keep track of the clues.

As you read the following passage, ask yourself what the writer might be implying about the government of the Soviet Union. Then answer the question that follows.

> When the Soviets shot down a Korean airliner, they claimed that the airliner was a spy plane. When Soviet leaders die, the public gets no information about the process of selecting a new leader. And when a terrible nuclear accident occurred in the Soviet Union, the Soviet government's initial reaction was to pretend that nothing had happened. The Soviet Union wants the rest of the world to mind its own business and leave the Soviets alone.

▶ The author believes that the Soviet government

(1) doesn't keep secrets from the rest of the world
(2) wants to improve relations with the West
(3) is very thoughtful and careful
(4) wants to conquer the world
(5) tries to keep its actions secret

You were right if you chose (5), *tries to keep its actions secret*. The writer gives three pieces of evidence:

● the fear that the Korean airliner was spying on them,

● the secret process of choosing Soviet leaders, and

● the Soviets' attempt to keep the nuclear accident a secret.

Putting the evidence together, you can see that the passage implies that secrecy is very important to the Soviet government. You can eliminate the other answers because there is no evidence for them in the passage.

## EXERCISE 4: INFERRING OPINIONS

*Directions:* Read each passage carefully. Answer the questions that follow each passage, making sure you have found evidence for the answer you choose.

> Franklin D. Roosevelt, president of the U.S. in the 1930s, was crippled by polio. However, most Americans did not realize the extent of his handicap. FDR never discussed his health problems in public, and he was careful to show as few signs of his handicap as possible. The press also helped him by not calling attention to his physical problems. His strategy was so successful that his handicap did not prevent him from being re-elected president three times.

1. Why did President Roosevelt want to keep people from being very aware of his handicap?

   **(1)** He wanted people to believe he was healthy enough to keep up with his responsibilities.
   **(2)** He didn't want to hurt his social life.
   **(3)** He didn't want to be reelected.
   **(4)** He enjoyed fooling the American public.
   **(5)** He wanted to find out how powerful the press could be in shaping public opinion.

Thousands of elderly Japanese men and women are experiencing difficult times. Once, the Japanese were known for their tradition of responsibility and care for their elders. Now most Japanese say that they don't feel they should have to support their aging parents.

Similarly, older parents don't want to get in the way or be a financial burden to their children. Parents also may find it hard to accept their children's modern lifestyles, making them difficult housemates. As a result, many older Japanese live alone on limited incomes.

2. The passage suggests that, in the past, older Japanese were

   **(1)** ready to die at sixty-five
   **(2)** willing to accept their children's lifestyle changes
   **(3)** living alone on limited incomes
   **(4)** supported by their children
   **(5)** saving money so that they could support themselves in retirement

3. The Japanese will have to find a new way to

   **(1)** make children support their parents when they are old
   **(2)** help elderly people die when they are ready
   **(3)** ensure that older people are taken care of
   **(4)** teach older people the modern lifestyles of young Japanese
   **(5)** make sure that older people can live alone on limited incomes

**Doonesbury**                                    BY GARRY TRUDEAU

**4.** The comic strip is written from the point of view of

(1) a newspaper reporter
(2) president of the United States
(3) a father
(4) a child
(5) a project planner for Star Wars

**5.** It is the cartoonist's opinion that

(1) Star Wars will lead to world peace
(2) we should build a peace shield to stop missiles in outer space
(3) we should listen more to children
(4) television is the best medium of communication
(5) Star Wars can't really protect us

**Answers start on page 206.**

# Expressing Opinion in Political Cartoons

A political cartoon expresses the opinion of the artist. Usually political cartoons comment on current events. One key to understanding most political cartoons is background knowledge of what was going on in the world when the cartoon was created. In this book, you'll be given background clues to the cartoons.

Another key to understanding political cartoons is symbols. A symbol stands for something—for example, a dollar sign ($) stands for money. Political cartoons often use symbols.

A third key to understanding political cartoons is understanding the titles and all the labels. Always read every word on a cartoon. Notice especially when words label a particular figure or part of the cartoon. For example, the title of the following cartoon is especially important.

**Background clues:** In the early 1800s, the Massachusetts legislature, controlled by Governor Gerry, created an oddly shaped voting district. The shape of this new district was designed to help Governor Gerry keep control of the legislature.

## The Gerry-mander.

*A new species of Monster, which appeared in Essex South District in January last.*

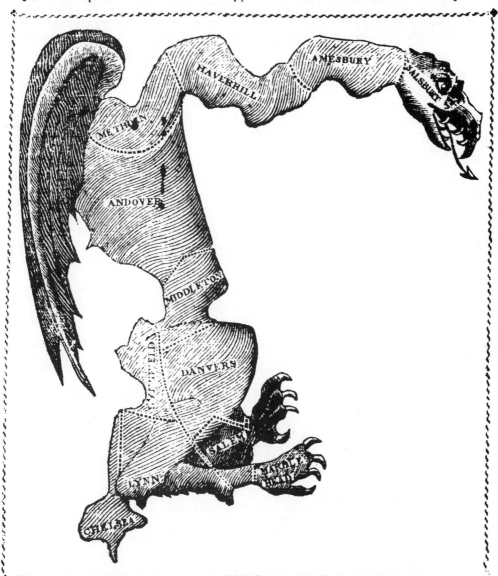

▶ What does the cartoonist call the animal in the cartoon? _____

The animal is called the Gerry-mander.

▶ Whom is the cartoonist criticizing? _____

He is criticizing Governor Gerry. You know this because he called the animal the *Gerry*-mander.

▶ The cartoonist's opinion is that the Essex South District boundaries are

**(1)** a major creative accomplishment
**(2)** a good example of democracy at work
**(3)** drawn unfairly
**(4)** drawn in the shape of an animal
**(5)** drawn fairly

You were correct if you chose (3), *drawn unfairly*. The cartoonist is criticizing Gerry for reshaping a voting district for his own advantage.

   In this cartoon, the Gerry-mander monster symbolizes the voting district whose lines were drawn for Gerry's benefit. The term *gerrymander* is still in use today. Politicians changing the boundaries of voting districts to their own advantage are accused of *gerrymandering*.

---

### Cartoon Tip

One of the most commonly used symbols in political cartoons is Uncle Sam. He stands for the United States. Uncle Sam is usually a tall man with white hair and a beard, wearing clothes with stars and stripes on them.

---

## EXERCISE 5: ANALYZING POLITICAL CARTOONS

*Directions:* Study each cartoon and its background clues; then answer the questions that follow.

**Background clues:** The United States is a very strong and active military power, with military bases all over the world.

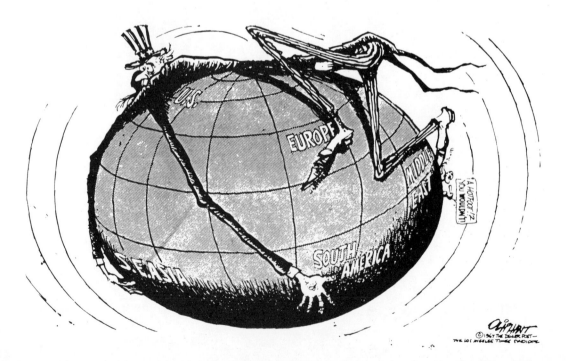

**1.** What does the cartoonist use as a symbol for the United States?

_____

**2.** What is the cartoon character trying to do?

_____

**3.** The cartoonist's opinion is that the United States

    **(1)** should act as the policeman of the world
    **(2)** cannot control the entire world
    **(3)** should increase its military budget
    **(4)** is the world's last hope against communism
    **(5)** is not doing enough to fight world hunger

**Background clues:** After the Civil War, New York City politics were controlled by a political organization called Tammany Hall. The boss of Tammany Hall was William Tweed.

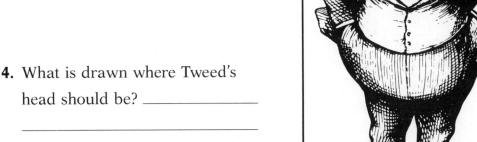

THE "BRAINS"

**4.** What is drawn where Tweed's head should be? _____

_____

**5.** What does the artist think Boss Tweed uses instead of brains?

_____

**6.** The cartoonist's main point is that Boss Tweed

    **(1)** is an honest man who works for a living
    **(2)** is a banker
    **(3)** eats too much
    **(4)** is corrupt
    **(5)** is a wealthy man

**Background clues:** This cartoon was drawn at a time when the U.S. economy was starting to recover from a recession.

7. What is the name of the big fighter sitting in the corner?

_____

8. What is the name of the skinny fighter knocked out on the floor?

_____

9. In the opinion of this cartoonist, taxes

   **(1)** must increase to save the economy
   **(2)** are knocking out the economic recovery
   **(3)** will help the boxing industry
   **(4)** must be collected for the health of the economy
   **(5)** are hurting boxers

**Answers start on page 206.**

# HYPOTHESES IN SOCIAL STUDIES

## Distinguishing Fact from Hypothesis

Sometimes an author gives the cause of an event or a trend as a statement of fact, as in the following example:

> Ponda did not get to work on time because her car broke down.

*Effect:* Ponda did not get to work on time.
*Cause (fact):* because her car broke down

Sometimes, however, a writer is not sure of the cause of an event, but he makes a good educated guess. We call this guess a **hypothesis**. The writer in the following example gives a hypothesis for why something happened.

> Our son Larry called just two days before our fortieth anniversary. We were surprised that he did not mention the anniversary. Then we realized that possibly he was planning a surprise party.

*Effect:* Larry did not mention the anniversary.
*Possible Cause (hypothesis):* He was planning a surprise party.

### EXERCISE 6: DISTINGUISHING FACT FROM HYPOTHESIS

*Directions:* Each of the following sentences describes a cause-and-effect relationship. Write *F* in the blank if the cause is stated as a fact. Write *H* in the blank if the cause is stated as a hypothesis.

*Example:* __H__ The widespread use of air conditioning may have made economic growth possible in the Southeast.

_____ 1. The cause of the Air India crash was the explosion of a terrorist bomb.

_____ 2. As a result of six months of intensive counseling, the Martins decided not to file for divorce.

_____ 3. It is possible that President Reagan's acting experience has helped him win votes.

_____ 4. Research suggests that brain damage in criminals may be a cause of violent crime.

**Answers start on page 206.**

# Identifying a Hypothesis

In a social studies passage, an author will often state a cause as a possibility, or hypothesis, rather than as a fact. It is important to recognize when authors are stating facts and when they are suggesting a hypothesis. In the following example, notice that the author does not know for sure why leaders are supporting basic education. But she does give you a possible explanation.

> All over the country, both labor and business leaders are supporting efforts to provide basic education to adults. These leaders may feel that workers will need this basic education in order to get and keep jobs in the future.

▶ According to the passage, what is the most likely cause of the efforts of labor and business leaders to educate adults?

(1) They feel a new spirit of charity.
(2) They want workers to be able to vote in union elections.
(3) In the future, workers will need to have a basic education.
(4) They recognize that labor and business must work together.
(5) They are concerned about a lack of workers for unskilled jobs.

You were right if you chose (3). The author says, "These leaders may feel that workers will need this basic education in order to get and keep jobs in the future."

## EXERCISE 7: FINDING THE AUTHOR'S HYPOTHESIS

*Directions:* Read each passage and answer the questions that follow.

> To middle-class Americans, the main purpose of a house is not simply protection from the weather. Instead, a house is an investment. To many, the most important feature of a house is its possible resale value. The focus on resale value has brought about changes in houses. For example, in 1900, only the richest families had two bathrooms in their houses. Now two- and three-bathroom houses are common because the extra bathrooms increase the resale value of a house.

1. Why does the author think that two- and three-bathroom houses are now common in the United States?

(1) Many families have more servants.
(2) Many families are larger.
(3) Extra bathrooms increase the resale value of a home.
(4) Americans have settled down and now have enough time to make additions to their homes.
(5) The homes are designed to house more than one family.

In the United States, we have one lawyer for every 440 people. Former Supreme Court Chief Justice Warren Burger once said, "We may well be on our way to a society overrun by hordes of lawyers, hungry as locusts, and brigades of judges in numbers never before contemplated." Why do we have so many lawyers? It may be because every college graduate who wants to get rich thinks that becoming a lawyer is the way to do it.

**2.** How does the author of the passage explain why there are so many lawyers in the United States?

**(1)** We are trying to stay ahead of the Russians.
**(2)** We are trying to control a wave of crime.
**(3)** There are many dedicated people who want to help others solve their problems.
**(4)** Many people think law is a good way to make money.
**(5)** The United States has the best law schools in the world.

Credit union members are more likely to save money than customers of regular banks. Credit union officials think they know why. Credit union members can have part of their paychecks set aside automatically in a savings account. Credit union officials think that their members are less likely to spend money that they never saw in the first place. In this way, their savings build up.

**3.** How do credit union officials explain the high rate of savings among their members?

**(1)** The members bank at regular banks also.
**(2)** The credit unions encourage them to save through advertising.
**(3)** Credit union officials encourage people who don't want to save money to bank elsewhere.
**(4)** Credit unions pay a higher rate of interest on savings accounts.
**(5)** Members won't spend money that they never see in the first place.

**Answers start on page 207.**

# Developing a Hypothesis

Sometimes a writer leaves it up to you to figure something out. The writer might describe an event or a trend without explaining why it happened. You can often use the evidence in the passage along with your common sense to develop a hypothesis to explain something. Try the following example:

"We almost had to push the healthier, lighter foods on employees a couple of years ago," recalled Joseph P. Kingrey, president of ARA Services' Business Dining Division. "Lately, it's become a craze."

Indeed, corporate dining facilities are picking up on the same trends that have swept through expensive restaurants. A recent study by the National Restaurant Association indicates that decaffeinated coffee, fresh fruit, and main dish salads are among the fastest growing items in restaurants.

▶ A possible cause of the increased popularity of main dish salads is

**(1)** people want to spend less on food
**(2)** a shortage of high-quality chicken and beef
**(3)** people are tired of hamburgers and steaks
**(4)** people have become more concerned about their health
**(5)** a new, better tasting lettuce has been developed

You were correct if you chose (4). The passage suggests this explanation in several ways. Healthier, lighter foods have become a craze, and decaffeinated coffee and fresh fruit are becoming more popular. You can put this evidence together and conclude that a likely reason for the salads being more popular is that they are healthier. There's no evidence in the passage for the other choices.

## EXERCISE 8: MAKING A REASONABLE HYPOTHESIS

*Directions:* Read each passage and answer the questions that follow.

Mel Fisher first heard about two treasure ships that sank in 1622 in a book called *The Treasure Hunter's Guide.* In 1970, Fisher began a sixteen-year search of the ocean floor near Florida, looking for the ships. Fisher had to raise money from 1,200 investors to pay for the costly search. He finally found one of the ships in 1986. It held a treasure of over $400 million worth of jewels and precious metals.

1. Which of the following hypotheses best explains why Mel Fisher was looking for the ships?

   **(1)** He wanted to know how ships were built in the 1600s.
   **(2)** He wanted to publish a book on the dangers of shipping in the 1600s.
   **(3)** He wanted the valuable treasure from the ships.
   **(4)** He was doing research for his book, *The Treasure Hunter's Guide.*
   **(5)** He was working for a group of investors.

Few people today pay directly for their medical care. Instead, they have health insurance, such as Blue Cross/Blue Shield. For more than a generation, the cost of health insurance has been rising very fast. The health insurance companies say that customers go to doctors and hospitals more often now than they did in the past. This makes health insurance more expensive.

2. Which of the following might explain why people visit doctors more now than in the past?

   (1) The cost is paid for by insurance, so people are more willing to see doctors.
   (2) People feel that doctors now have less awareness of patient needs.
   (3) People have more diseases now than they did in the past.
   (4) Health insurance has become very expensive, so people avoid over-using it.
   (5) Blue Cross/Blue Shield encourages its customers to go to doctors often.

In 1967 the Field Foundation paid a group of doctors to study hunger and malnutrition in certain areas of the United States. These doctors found that many people in the United States were going hungry.

Ten years later, the foundation sent another group of doctors to the same areas. The second group of doctors reported that food aid programs (such as food stamps) had helped people in those regions. In 1967, the doctors had seen many children with swollen stomachs, dull eyes, and open wounds. In 1977, they saw fewer signs of hunger and its related illnesses.

3. In 1967, what was the probable cause of the poor physical condition of many children?

   (1) They were too dependent on handouts from the government.
   (2) They were being neglected by their parents.
   (3) They lived in unsanitary conditions.
   (4) They did not have enough good food.
   (5) There were not enough doctors.

**Answers start on page 207.**

# PREDICTING AN OUTCOME

## What Could Happen?

All actions lead to outcomes, some of which you can reasonably predict. Just as you can apply your reading and reasoning skills to recognize a possible cause, you can use these skills to recognize a possible outcome.

The manager of a supermarket advertised a sale on milk, eggs, and orange juice. Check each of the following that are likely outcomes of advertising the sale.

a. _____ The store may sell more orange juice than usual.
b. _____ Employees may be more likely to steal eggs.
c. _____ The store may order extra milk from its supplier.
d. _____ Business at the store may decline overall.

Did you check *a* and *c*? The store would probably sell more orange juice since the price is lower. The store probably would also order extra milk, since larger quantities might be sold at the sale price.

## EXERCISE 9: IDENTIFYING PROBABLE OUTCOMES

*Directions:* Put a check in the blank in front of each likely outcome.

1. The day-care center is starting a program to have senior citizens volunteer to help care for the babies.

_____ a. The babies may get less attention.
_____ b. The day-care center may have to charge more for caring for babies.
_____ c. The babies may be touched and held more often.
_____ d. The senior citizens may feel that their help is needed.

2. Sheila just got promoted from a part-time job as a typist to a full-time job as a secretary.

_____ a. Sheila may see her preschool children more than she did before.
_____ b. Sheila may improve her office skills.
_____ c. Sheila may be happier about her future.
_____ d. Sheila may be able to buy her children new clothes.
_____ e. Sheila may have more time to clean her house.

**Answers start on page 207.**

# Identifying the Author's Prediction

As you have seen, we cannot always be certain of the result of something. However, a writer will often try to predict the outcome of an action or a trend. In this section, you'll practice identifying predictions in a passage.

In the following example paragraph, look for the prediction the author is making. Answer the question that follows the paragraph.

> Several states have recently raised the legal drinking age to twenty-one. Lawmakers say that making drinking illegal for eighteen- to twenty-year-olds will help prevent accidents caused by drunken drivers. They argue that younger drinkers are more likely to take chances. However, I feel that making drinking illegal for this age group will increase accidents caused by drunken driving. If eighteen- to twenty-year-olds are kept out of bars, they will drink right in their cars.

▶ What does the writer predict will be the outcome of raising the drinking age to twenty-one?

**(1)** Accidents caused by drunken drivers will decrease.
**(2)** Fewer teenagers will drink.
**(3)** Bars will still allow eighteen- to twenty-year-olds to drink.
**(4)** Eighteen- to twenty-year-olds will stop drinking.
**(5)** More accidents will be caused by drunken drivers.

You were right if you chose (5). The author says that raising the drinking age will increase accidents caused by drunken driving.

## EXERCISE 10: IDENTIFYING THE AUTHOR'S PREDICTION

*Directions:* Read each passage and answer the questions that follow.

> Colleges and universities have to adjust to changing times. For years, the vast majority of students at these schools were in their late teens and early twenties. Those age groups are now declining in numbers. Many schools are responding to this trend by trying to bring in older students. The colleges' only other choice is to enroll fewer students and become smaller. Few colleges, however, are likely to take that road.

**1.** The author predicts that colleges and universities will

    **(1)** become smaller as less students enroll
    **(2)** turn to the federal government for help
    **(3)** have many more older students
    **(4)** branch out into other businesses
    **(5)** encourage students to graduate from high school at an earlier age

Thomas Jefferson thought that small farmers were the most valuable members of society. Jefferson would be disappointed by what's happening in agriculture today. Large farms are the most common type now, and small farms are getting rarer. This trend is likely to continue. In the future, farms will get larger and larger, and small farms will continue to disappear.

2. What is the current trend in the size of farms?

   **(1)** Most farms are small.
   **(2)** Small farms are becoming more and more rare.
   **(3)** Large farms are becoming more efficient.
   **(4)** The government is buying up small family farms.
   **(5)** Fewer and fewer farms are large.

3. The author expects that

   **(1)** there will be larger farms in the future
   **(2)** a popular movement will lead to more small farms
   **(3)** the number and size of farms will become stable
   **(4)** the government will step in to save the family farm
   **(5)** many large farms will fail to survive

Businesses are feeling pressure from many sides to help fill the needs of working parents. Many companies are allowing either mothers or fathers to go on leave when a new baby is born. Other companies are helping parents make child-care arrangements. A few companies are opening day-care centers in the workplace. These centers are still rare, but they will certainly become more common in the future.

4. The author predicts that

   **(1)** day-care centers will become less common
   **(2)** fathers will not be allowed to take leaves when their babies are born
   **(3)** more mothers will stay home with their children in the future
   **(4)** businesses will become less concerned with the needs of working parents
   **(5)** day-care centers in the workplace will become more common

**Answers start on page 207.**

# Making a Prediction Based on a Passage

Many times an author gives enough information in a passage so that you can make your own predictions. Be careful to back up your predictions with evidence from the passage. Read the following passage carefully. Choose the answer to the question, basing your choice on the information that is given.

> Computers are everywhere now. Many adults—in the workplace, in school, at home—are struggling to learn the basics of computer operation. In addition, public schools have acquired computers and made them available to children. Soon almost all schoolchildren in the United States will get a lot of experience using computers, both in school and out.

▶ A likely result of children's using computers in school is that

(1) they will need less computer training when they are adults
(2) they will become bored by computers and never use them again
(3) the computer fad will fade as computers are overused
(4) schools will depend on computers to take over the role of the teacher
(5) they will learn nothing but how to use computers

The correct answer is choice (1). If all children have a lot of experience using computers, they will not need an introduction to computers when they are adults.

## EXERCISE 11: MAKING A PREDICTION BASED ON A PASSAGE

*Directions:* Read each passage and answer the questions that follow.

> Bolivia is, by almost any standard, the most desperate country in the world. New economic problems are now surfacing alongside its longer-term political woes.
>
> Last autumn, the world tin market collapsed. Bolivia's tin mines are closed now. Then the winter crash in oil prices hurt the natural gas business, Bolivia's other legal source of foreign trade. The cocaine business is booming, but the government barely avoided a civil war in January because of it.
>
> The result has been one of the worst inflations in recent history. The value of a $5,000 bank note has shrunk to 50 cents in three years.

1. Which of the following actions could the U.S. government take to assist Bolivia?

    **(1)** sell oil and natural gas to Bolivia
    **(2)** declare war on Bolivia
    **(3)** send large shipments of tin to Bolivia
    **(4)** help Bolivia start new industries
    **(5)** borrow money from Bolivia

2. Bolivia's economy could improve as a result of

    **(1)** a rise in world tin prices
    **(2)** drug users cutting down on cocaine use
    **(3)** a drop in oil prices
    **(4)** an increase in natural gas production in the United States
    **(5)** an increase in the rate of inflation in Bolivia

    The Choctaw Indians in Mississippi have brought jobs to their people. The unemployment rate for the tribe has dropped from 45 percent to below 20 percent. The tribe convinced several large companies to build plants on the reservation where the Choctaw live. Now the Indians operate and work in plants that assemble radios, make wire harnesses for cars, and put finishing details on greeting cards.

    Tribal leaders say that now the Choctaw won't have to leave the reservation to find jobs. They have good opportunities right there.

3. As a result of the new plants on the reservation, Choctaw young people are likely to

    **(1)** leave school to work at unskilled jobs in the plants
    **(2)** stay on the reservation but remain unemployed
    **(3)** become better educated to prepare for good jobs
    **(4)** spend more time learning traditional Indian arts
    **(5)** realize how much better off they are than youth in cities

**Answers start on page 207.**

## EXERCISE 12: CHAPTER REVIEW

*Directions:* Read each passage and answer the questions that follow.

Questions 1–2 are based on the following passage.

*This passage is about Calvin Coolidge, who was president of the United States from 1923 to 1929.*

> The sudden thrust of the Presidential mantle about his thin shoulders staggered him for a time. He really was a timid person those first few days. He promised to carry on the Harding policies—whatever that might mean—and then lapsed into silence for a month.
>
> During that month he was built into a myth. It was one of the greatest feats of newspaper propaganda that the modern world has seen. It really was a miracle. He said nothing. Newspapers must have copy. So we grasped at little incidents to build up human interest stories and we created a character. He kept his counsel. Therefore he was a strong and silent man. The editorial writers on newspapers which were satisfied with the status quo, the big Eastern journals, created the strong, silent man. Then, in time, as the country found out he was not a superman, neither strong nor silent, they emphasized his little witticisms, his dry wit, and we had a national character—Cal. Everybody spoke of him fondly as "Cal." He was one of us. He was the ordinary man incarnate.

1. Why did the newspapers make up a strong, silent image for President Coolidge?

   **(1)** They admired his strong, silent style of leadership.
   **(2)** They believed silence was a virtue.
   **(3)** The real Coolidge didn't give them anything to write about.
   **(4)** They wanted to make sure the American people understood him.
   **(5)** They wanted to create a miracle.

2. What was the truth about the images of Coolidge?

   **(1)** Calvin Coolidge was a master of public relations when he created his image of "Cal."
   **(2)** The real Calvin Coolidge was different from the public image of him.
   **(3)** Calvin Coolidge was willing to dig for the truth.
   **(4)** Calvin Coolidge was a strong and silent man.
   **(5)** Calvin Coolidge's inspired leadership and great sense of humor have made him one of our most remembered presidents.

Questions 3–4 are based on the following bar graph.

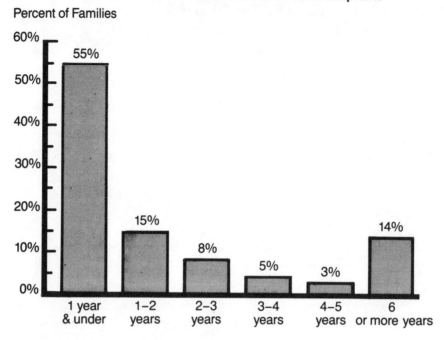

**Time on Welfare for Massachusetts AFDC Recipients**

3. According to the graph, how long do more than half of Massachusetts welfare recipients stay on welfare?

(1) 1 year or less
(2) 1–2 years
(3) 3–4 years
(4) 4–5 years
(5) 6 or more years

4. Given the information on the chart, it seems that most people go on welfare

(1) in order to collect benefits for their entire lives
(2) so that they can afford to have more babies
(3) to help them get back on their feet at a difficult time
(4) to avoid their duties as parents
(5) so that they never have to work again

Questions 5–6 are based on the following cartoon.

**Background clues:** The news media focuses a lot of attention on stories about terrorists, especially when they take hostages.

**5.** The terrorist in the cartoon says, "Shoot or I'll stop!" Whom is he talking to? _____

**6.** What is the cartoonist's opinion of terrorist actions?

   **(1)** Terrorists are daring and courageous.
   **(2)** Terrorists want their hostages to suffer.
   **(3)** Their actions reduce the number of American tourists traveling abroad.
   **(4)** Terrorists are using the news media to get attention.
   **(5)** News reporting about terrorist actions is biased.

     Since the Charleston became popular in the 1920s, America has been swept by a series of dance fads. Jitterbugging, the twist, and, more recently, disco and breakdancing all burst onto the music scene and then faded.

**7.** A reasonable prediction based on this paragraph would be

   **(1)** the Charleston is due for a comeback
   **(2)** there will be another dance fad in the next few years
   **(3)** dance crazes will become a thing of the past
   **(4)** older people will be learning to breakdance
   **(5)** the next popular dance will start in Japan

A juicy state governor's race pitted a popular Democratic governor, Michael Dukakis, against two Republicans who hoped to take over his job. However, the Republican candidates had a few problems. Over 1,000 signatures on Greg Hyatt's nominating petitions were found to be forgeries. Then the other Republican candidate, Royall Switzler, admitted that he had lied about his military record and withdrew from the race.

8. Based on the information in the passage, it is reasonable to expect that

   **(1)** Greg Hyatt will win the election for governor
   **(2)** Royall Switzler will win the election for governor
   **(3)** Michael Dukakis will win the election for governor
   **(4)** the race for governor will be too close to call
   **(5)** the Democrats will have trouble raising money for the governor's race

Questions 9–10 are based on the following passage.

Home prices are soaring in Tristan. The increase cannot be blamed on inflation, since prices in general are increasing by only 4 percent per year. Similar cities are not having an unusual rise in the price of homes. The population of Tristan is growing very slowly, so there is no housing shortage to blame the prices on.

However, there may be a psychological explanation for the dramatic increase in home prices. Prices may be going up because people expect them to go up. Buyers will pay a high price for a house if they believe that someone else will pay even more for it when they are ready to sell.

In the late 1970s, the same thing happened in California. Eventually people stopped buying homes because the prices got so high, and prices leveled off. The same thing will probably happen soon in Tristan.

9. What does the author think is the cause of Tristan's rapidly rising housing prices?

   **(1)** high employment
   **(2)** a housing shortage caused by large numbers of people moving to Tristan
   **(3)** higher construction costs increasing the cost of a new home
   **(4)** high inflation
   **(5)** people paying high prices because they think the prices will go even higher

**10.** What does the author believe will happen to the price of Tristan housing soon?

**(1)** Prices will level off.
**(2)** There will be a crash, with prices declining rapidly.
**(3)** Prices will continue to increase rapidly.
**(4)** Prices will begin to swing up and down.
**(5)** After a brief decline, prices will increase rapidly again.

In 1940, only 8 percent of black men earned more money than the average white man. By 1980, 29 percent of employed black men earned more money than the average white man.

What brought about this dramatic change? One study examined several major factors: education, the migration of blacks from the South to the North, blacks moving from rural areas into cities, welfare programs, and affirmative action programs. The study concluded that when blacks moved to cities they had better opportunities. However, education enabled blacks to take advantage of these opportunities. Education was the key factor that allowed blacks to succeed.

**11.** What do the authors of the study believe is the best way to improve the standard of living of black people?

**(1)** provide educational opportunities
**(2)** encourage relocation in the South
**(3)** maintain affirmative action programs
**(4)** ensure that there is good medical care
**(5)** encourage migration to urban areas

**Answers start on page 207.**

## CHAPTER REVIEW EVALUATION CHART

| Reading Skill | Question Numbers* | Review Pages | Number Correct |
|---|---|---|---|
| Reading a Bar Graph | 3 | 62–63 | _____ /1 |
| Fact/Opinion | **5**, **6**, 11 | 114–116, 122–126 | _____ /3 |
| Inference | 1, 2 | 117–122 | _____ /2 |
| Hypotheses | **4**, 9 | 127–131 | _____ /2 |
| Predicting Outcomes | 7, 8, 10 | 132–136 | _____ /3 |

*Question numbers in **dark type** are based on illustrations.

Your score: _____ out of 11. Passing score: 7 out of 11.

# 5
# Evaluating Social Studies Materials

In this chapter, you will learn to evaluate what you read. When you evaluate, you ask yourself whether something is logical. You will practice judging whether you have enough information to answer a question or solve a problem and whether the information you have is what you need. You will also practice identifying errors in reasoning. And you'll practice recognizing the values that have an effect on beliefs, decision making, and action. Also, you'll learn what propaganda is and how to recognize it.

# DO YOU HAVE ENOUGH INFORMATION?

## Using the Information in a Passage

Every day you evaluate whether you have enough information to solve a problem or answer someone's question. Sometimes when you're reading a passage in social studies, you have to do the same thing. You must figure out whether you have enough information to answer a question or make a decision. Read the example paragraph carefully, then decide whether you have enough information to prove the following statements.

> It was 3:00 A.M. Larry was driving at eighty miles per hour on the interstate in his 1987 Oldsmobile. An hour before, he had noticed that his gas gauge was on "Empty" as he passed a closed gas station. Suddenly, his engine stopped and his car slowly rolled to a stop.

Put a check in front of each statement that the passage gives you enough information to prove.

_____ **1.** Larry's car had engine trouble.

_____ **2.** Larry's car had run out of gas.

_____ **3.** Larry was coming home from his night job.

**1.** Not enough information. It is possible that he had engine trouble, since the passage states that the engine stopped, but you can't tell for sure.

**2.** Enough information. He had driven at eighty miles per hour for an hour with the fuel gauge on "Empty."

**3.** Not enough information. It is possible, but there is not enough information in the passage for proof.

## EXERCISE 1: IS THERE ENOUGH INFORMATION?

*Directions:* Following each passage are four statements. Put a check (✔) in front of each statement that can be proven by using the information in the passage. Put an *X* in front of each statement that cannot be proven based on the passage.

> All fourteen Southern states allow the death penalty. In 1984 in those fourteen states, there were a total of 755 prisoners waiting for execution. Of the thirty-six states outside the South, twenty-three allow the death penalty. In 1984 those twenty-three states had 447 prisoners on death row.

_____ **1.** In 1984 there were more prisoners on death row in the fourteen southern States than in all thirty-six other states.

_____ **2.** In 1984 New York had fewer prisoners on death row than Florida.

_____ **3.** Murder is increasing in the southern United States.

_____ **4.** A person convicted of murder in any southern state could be given the death penalty.

When people talk about the "heartland" of America, they usually mean the Midwest. Some researchers have decided that the "typical American voter" lives in Dayton, a service and manufacturing city on the Miami River in southwestern Ohio. This typical American voter is a housewife whose husband is a machinist—perhaps with National Cash Register or with Frigidaire—and whose brother-in-law is a policeman. She considers herself a Democrat but often votes Republican.

Companies that want to find out what products people will buy also believe that the Midwest is typical. Columbus, Ohio, boasts that companies like to test-market new products there because it offers such a good cross section of the country.

_____ **5.** The typical American voter likes to try new products.

_____ **6.** Many companies believe that, if a new product is successful in Columbus, it will be successful in the nation as a whole.

_____ **7.** The "typical American voter" lives in a city.

_____ **8.** Ohio will always be the home of the typical American voter.

**Answers start on page 208.**

# Using the Information on a Map

A map might not always have all the information you need to answer a question. See what information you can get from the following map.

Does the map of Vermont provide enough information to prove the following statements? Put a check (✓) in the blank in front of the statement you can prove. Put an X in front of the statement you can't prove.

_____ The capital of Vermont is Montpelier.

_____ Potatoes are produced in Vermont.

You were right if you put an X in front of the first statement. If you look carefully at the map, you will see a few cities, but not Montpelier. You have no way of knowing whether this is true or not. You should have put a check in front of the second statement. Scanning the map, you will see several spots where potatoes are produced.

## EXERCISE 2: USING INFORMATION ON A MAP

*Directions:* Following each map are several statements. In the blank in front of each statement, put a check (✓) if there is enough information on the map to prove the statement true. Put an X if there is not enough information.

Questions 1–3 are based on the Vermont products map on page 144.

_____ **1.** Maple syrup is produced in Vermont.

_____ **2.** Dairy products are Vermont's major source of farm income.

_____ **3.** New Hampshire borders Vermont.

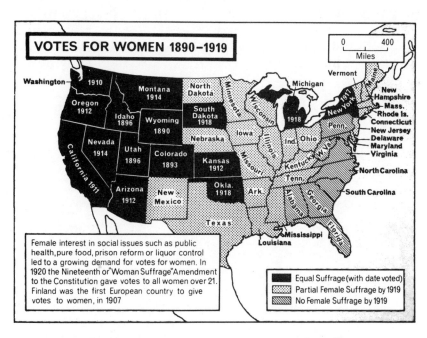

_____ **4.** In general, the western states gave equal suffrage to women before the rest of the country.

_____ **5.** Pennsylvania (Penn.) did not allow any female suffrage by 1919.

_____ **6.** More women lived in New York in 1917 than in any other state.

**Answers start on page 208.**

# THE RIGHT INFORMATION

## Looking for the Right Facts

Doreen is a feminist—a supporter of women's rights. When she went to vote in the primary for state senator, she found that Marie Home was running against Tom Taylor. Doreen voted for Marie because she was a woman. She later found out that it was Tom, not Marie, who supported the women's issues that were important to her.

Doreen made an error many of us make: she wanted a certain result, but she used the wrong information to make an important decision. She wanted a state senator who would support women's issues. She thought that all she needed to know was which candidate was a woman. Unfortunately, her choice went against her desire to have a state senator who would support women's rights.

## Irrelevant Information

Irrelevant information isn't really related to the subject being talked about. Sometimes writers try to persuade you to do something by giving you irrelevant but appealing information. Study the following advertisement. Think about what the advertiser wants you to do and what reasons you are given to do it.

**WIN THE LARGEST SWEEPSTAKES OF ITS KIND IN AMERICA!**

If you are the lucky winner, Ed McMahon of the "Tonight Show" will hand you your winning check on national TV.
We also offer the lowest prices on your favorite magazines!

ORDER THESE GREAT MAGAZINES FROM US TODAY!!!

What does the advertiser want you to do?

_____

What irrelevant reasons are given for doing it?

_____

The purpose of the ad is to convince you to buy magazines. However, the facts that this is the largest sweepstakes of its kind in America and that Ed McMahon will be handing the winner the check are both poor reasons to buy the magazines. Neither reason has anything to do with the magazines! However, getting your favorite magazine at the lowest price is a good reason to buy the magazines.

# EXERCISE 3: IDENTIFYING IRRELEVANT INFORMATION

*Directions:* Read each passage. First, figure out what the writer wants you to do. Then fill in the reasons that are not relevant to the decision you must make.

**Passage 1**

Dear Editor,

I want to urge your readers to vote for Gil Cohen for mayor. Everyone agrees that he is more attractive than his opponent. He has years of administrative experience, much more than the other candidate. He has promised to increase the police budget in order to control crime. Finally, people should vote for him because he has spent over $100,000 of his own money to get elected.

Sincerely,
Bernice Cohen

**a.** What does the writer want her readers to do?

_____

**b.** What irrelevant reasons for doing it does she give?

_____

**Passage 2**

My committee hopes that the contract for building the K9 missile will be given to the General Progress Corporation of California. General Progress has years of experience as a defense contractor. It has a record of finishing its contracts on time and under budget. Its home office is in my district, and General Progress has contributed generously to my reelection campaign. For all these reasons, General Progress is the best choice.

**a.** What does the writer want to convince his readers of?

_____

**b.** What irrelevant reasons does he give?

_____

**Answers start on page 208.**

## EXERCISE 4: USING INFORMATION CORRECTLY

*Directions:* Read each passage; then answer the questions that follow.

Many people outside the United States think of Americans as self-centered and selfish. Yet there is evidence for quite a different view. In 1985, Americans responded to the record "We Are the World" and the Live Aid concert by contributing millions of dollars to famine relief in Africa. A year later, Americans participated in Hands Across America, an event in which millions of people joined hands to raise millions of dollars more to feed hungry Americans.

1. Hands Across America was

   **(1)** a concert to benefit starving people in Africa
   **(2)** a record that featured America's most famous singers
   **(3)** an event that raised millions of dollars to feed hungry Americans
   **(4)** an event that proved that Americans were self-centered and selfish
   **(5)** an event that proved that Americans were willing to help needy people from other countries

2. There is enough proof in the passage to show that

   **(1)** the U.S. government is concerned with world hunger
   **(2)** Africa is successfully coping with its food problems
   **(3)** all musicians are concerned with helping others
   **(4)** Americans are becoming more self-centered
   **(5)** Americans can show generosity

In recent years, the United States has been divided sharply over the concept of affirmative action. For many years, minorities and women were kept out of jobs and schools because of their race or sex. Affirmative action programs try to correct past prejudice. Schools and employers using these programs search for qualified women and minorities to fill their openings.
Many Americans believe that hiring should not be influenced by race, sex, or religion. They insist that affirmative action is the wrong way of dealing with prejudice because it is prejudice working in reverse.

3. There is enough information to determine that

   **(1)** affirmative action programs have made up for past prejudice and are no longer needed
   **(2)** affirmative action is not fair to white males
   **(3)** affirmative action will not result in more black people in important jobs
   **(4)** affirmative action is an attempt to make up for past prejudice
   **(5)** affirmative action will be a major issue of the 1990s

The *kibbutz* is a bold social experiment being carried out in Israel. A kibbutz is a community in which most things are owned by everyone as a group. The kibbutz owns the land, all farm animals and equipment, and all crops. Sometimes it owns its own factories. In some kibbutzim, even the houses are owned by the community.

In some kibbutzim, people who are willing to give all they own to the kibbutz can be considered for membership, as long as they are under thirty-five years old. Older people are not allowed to join unless they marry a kibbutz member or their child is a kibbutz member. This ban on older people is a result of hard experience. People over thirty-five are usually set in their ways and unable to adjust to the needs of the kibbutz. After a very unpleasant period, older people usually drop out of the kibbutz, leaving anger and bitterness on both sides.

**4.** A kibbutz is a community in which

  **(1)** everybody must learn Hebrew, the language of Israel
  **(2)** new members must be over thirty-five years old
  **(3)** most things are owned in common
  **(4)** children cannot live with their parents
  **(5)** factories are owned by the richest people

**5.** A good reason for not allowing new members over thirty-five is

  **(1)** they have trouble adjusting to the kibbutz way of life
  **(2)** they will take advantage of the younger people
  **(3)** they cannot work as hard as younger people
  **(4)** they cannot give enough money to the kibbutz
  **(5)** they will try to take over the kibbutz and change all the rules

**Answers start on page 208.**

# ERRORS IN REASONING

In this chapter, you have already seen two sources of mistakes in reasoning: not having enough information and having the wrong kind of information. In this section, you will practice recognizing other errors in reasoning, such as

substituting personal beliefs, desires, or experience for facts:

"I have never gotten a parking ticket on this street; therefore, it must be legal to park here."

making general statements based on one example:

> "All those TV offers are rip-offs. My sister sent in $25 for a set of knives, and she never got it."

backward reasoning:

> "If all American voters are people over eighteen years old, then all people over eighteen years old are American voters."

Below are two reasons for a certain action. Put a check (✓) in front of the one that shows good reasoning. Put an X in front of the one that shows a reasoning error.

> Cali, the office manager, is trying to decide whether to purchase new word processing equipment for her office.

_____ The staff will get more work done if word processing equipment is purchased and used.

_____ She thinks the office ought to have the latest and most fancy equipment.

You should have put a check in front of the first reason. A good reason for purchasing new equipment is to improve productivity. You should have put an X in front of the second reason. This is an example of substituting a personal desire for good reasons.

## EXERCISE 5: RECOGNIZING ERRORS IN REASONING

*Directions:* Following each statement are two reasons for making a choice or taking an action. Put a check (✓) in the blank before the choice that shows good reasoning. Put an X in the blank before the choice that shows a reasoning error.

1. Sandy is planning to send his son Gary to college.

   _____ **a.** Since Sandy went to college, his son should go too.

   _____ **b.** Since Gary wants to become a doctor, he has to go to college.

2. Mel's Auto Body Shop is in financial trouble.

   _____ **a.** Since Mel's business has had an excellent financial record for thirty years, he is confident his bank will help him.

   _____ **b.** Since the government bailed out the Chrysler Corporation when it was in financial trouble, it will help out Mel's Auto Body Shop.

**3.** The Yellowbrick neighborhood decided not to work with the Froston Redevelopment Authority to improve the neighborhood.

_____ **a.** The Froston Redevelopment Authority wiped out the West End neighborhood thirty years ago. Therefore, the same thing will happen to the Yellowbrick neighborhood.

_____ **b.** Over thirty years, the Froston Redevelopment Authority has constantly ignored the wishes of Froston's neighborhoods. Instead, it has listened to wealthy developers. Therefore, it is risky to work with them.

**Answers start on page 209.**

# What Is the Problem Here?

It is important for you to be able to explain why reasoning is correct or why it is wrong. In the following exercise, you'll practice identifying and explaining reasoning problems. Try answering the questions based on the following cartoon.

**Background clues:** In the mid-1980s, people became very afraid of AIDS, an incurable, fatal disease.

▶ Why is the person in this cartoon fired? _____

▶ Why is it ridiculous that this person is getting fired? _____

The person is fired because his sister met a cab driver who has a cousin who knows someone with AIDS. It is ridiculous that he is getting fired because his connection with AIDS is so distant.

Now try some sample questions based on the following paragraph.

> A recent research study found that violent behavior might be caused by brain damage and child abuse. All the residents of death row spoken to by the researchers had some brain damage and had been abused in childhood. Because of the results of this study, we should put all brain-damaged people who have been victims of child abuse into mental hospitals.

▶ What does the author suggest should happen to people who have suffered child abuse and brain damage? _____

▶ What is the problem with his reasoning? _____

The author thinks that these people should be put into mental hospitals. His reasoning is poor because he is reasoning backward. The report stated that the violent people studied were brain-damaged and abused as children. That does not mean that *all* brain-damaged and abused people will be violent.

## EXERCISE 6: ERRORS IN REASONING

*Directions:* Answer the questions following each passage.

> In 1980, Ronald Reagan was running for president against President Jimmy Carter. He asked the voters if they were better off then than they were four years before. He suggested that, if they were worse off, they should vote for him to replace President Carter. I had had a hard year. My wife died, and my children dropped out of school. I started drinking and got fired from my job. I was doing much worse than four years before. Therefore, I voted for Ronald Reagan for president.

1. The writer of the passage decided to vote for Ronald Reagan because

   (1) he supported Reagan's economic policies
   (2) his life was going badly
   (3) he did not like Jimmy Carter
   (4) he felt that it was time for a change
   (5) he thought Reagan was a great speaker

2. What is the problem with his reasoning?_____

_____

I read about a study that found that, in general, married men are the happiest group of people. Unmarried women came in second in the happiness study. They were almost as happy with their lives as married men. Unmarried men finished third in the survey. Finally, the unhappiest group in the population was married women.

I am an unmarried woman. My husband left me five years ago, and I am still miserable as a result. Therefore, the study must be wrong. The unhappiest group of people are unmarried women.

**3.** The study found that the unhappiest group was

   **(1)** married men
   **(2)** married women
   **(3)** unmarried men
   **(4)** unmarried women
   **(5)** children

**4.** What is the problem with the speaker's reasoning?_____

_____

It is the role of government to protect its citizens from physical harm. Many Americans are injured or killed each year as a result of criminal activities. Many of these injuries are a result of the nationwide activities of organized crime. A proper and reasonable response to this situation is to have the Federal Bureau of Investigation (FBI) coordinate a nationwide effort to end organized crime.

**5.** The suggestion to have the FBI coordinate a nationwide effort to end organized crime is

   **(1)** a poor suggestion since the federal government should stay out of local affairs
   **(2)** a good suggestion since the FBI should be allowed to do anything it wants
   **(3)** a good suggestion since a national government agency should fight a national crime problem
   **(4)** a poor suggestion since local police officers can handle the job
   **(5)** a poor suggestion since not enough Americans are killed or injured by organized crime for the government to get involved

**Answers start on page 209.**

# RECOGNIZING VALUES

Everybody has values, those things that they consider important. We often think of the United States as a nation shaped by values. Many of the early settlers from Europe came to America for religious freedom. They valued their religion more than anything else. In the Declaration of Independence, Thomas Jefferson gave three values as the basis of the new nation: life, liberty, and the pursuit of happiness.

Many things you read and see express values. It is important to be able to recognize the values of the author or of the people the author writes about. Some people have values that you may think are noble, such as consideration for others or the importance of honesty. Other values can include wanting to make money, getting what you want no matter who gets hurt, concern for world peace, and patriotism. See if you can identify the values being expressed in the cartoon below.

**Background clues:** The National Rifle Association (NRA) opposes all gun control laws. They believe that all law-abiding Americans have the right to own and use guns.

▶ What value is being expressed by the shop owner in the cartoon?

**(1)** patriotism
**(2)** world peace
**(3)** human rights
**(4)** freedom to carry weapons
**(5)** consideration for others

The correct answer is choice (4), *freedom to carry weapons.* The caption shows that he will sell dangerous ammunition that is clearly not meant to be used against deer. The cartoon does not suggest choice (1), *patriotism.* His willingness to sell something so dangerous eliminates choices (2), (3), and (5).

## EXERCISE 7: RECOGNIZING VALUES

*Directions:* Study each passage or cartoon; then answer the questions that follow.

> In recent years, there has been controversy over the sale of the South African gold coin, the Krugerrand. Many people have bought the coins because they are made of pure gold. Other people have opposed the sale and purchase of Krugerrands in this country. They feel that the sale of Krugerrands helps support the current apartheid system in South Africa. They feel that by stopping the sale of Krugerrands they will exert pressure on the South African government to end the unequal treatment of whites and blacks.

1. According to the passage, what value is most important to those people buying Krugerrands?

   **(1)** supporting apartheid
   **(2)** making money
   **(3)** equality for all people
   **(4)** patriotism
   **(5)** world peace

2. According to the passage, what value is most important to those people opposing the sale of Krugerrands?

   **(1)** supporting apartheid
   **(2)** making money
   **(3)** equality for all people
   **(4)** patriotism
   **(5)** world peace

**Background clues:** The First Amendment to the U.S. Constitution guarantees freedom of the press. The men shown in this cartoon are President Reagan and some of his staff.

"I propose we reword the First Amendment and make it: FREEDOM FROM THE PRESS."

3. According to the cartoonist, what value is most important to President Reagan?

   **(1)** freedom of the press
   **(2)** making money
   **(3)** power of the president
   **(4)** solving America's problems
   **(5)** human rights

4. Based on this cartoon, what value seems to be most important to the cartoonist?

   **(1)** freedom of the press
   **(2)** making money
   **(3)** power of the presidency
   **(4)** solving America's problems
   **(5)** human rights

The New England town meeting has been called the purest form of democracy. At the meetings, every voter has the opportunity to "stand up and be counted" on issues that are important to the town. Any group coming to town meeting has the chance to appeal to the voters by speaking directly to them.

One town preservation society thought they had an issue that couldn't lose at town meeting. They wanted the town to buy an old farm and save the land for recreation and education. Everybody on the purchase committee wanted a chance to speak to the voters. By the fourth speaker, the voters were getting impatient.

Then a speaker opposed to the purchase argued that the farm cost too much to buy. He also pointed out that the Society had not estimated the costs of developing the land as a park or education center. How were the taxpayers to know what this purchase would cost in the long run?

Despite a poll of voters that showed them strongly in favor of saving open land, the proposed purchase of the farm was badly defeated.

5. What value of the voters did the town preservation society try to appeal to?

   **(1)** the need for efficiency
   **(2)** conservation of open land
   **(3)** the desire for lower taxes
   **(4)** the importance of communication
   **(5)** the spirit of fair play

6. The town preservation society was unsuccessful because

   **(1)** voters did not share the society's feeling about the importance of saving open land
   **(2)** voters wanted to lower their taxes
   **(3)** the purchase would not actually conserve any open land
   **(4)** voters were against increasing the recreational and educational resources of the town
   **(5)** voters were more concerned about the long-range costs than about conserving the land

**Answers start on page 209.**

# PROPAGANDA

## Propaganda in Daily Life

Propaganda presents a person, a product, or an idea as good or bad. Its purpose is to convince you. You see examples of propaganda every day. The most common example of propaganda is advertising. Does the following example look familiar?

---

**NEW MEDICAL BREAKTHROUGH!!!**

Lose up to 50 Pounds Without Dieting
EAT ALL YOUR FAVORITE FOODS AND STILL LOSE WEIGHT

---

All of us have seen these kinds of ads before. They pull at our emotions and desires. They tell us that we can look great without having to do any work for it. They tell only the good side of their products and leave out any possible harmful side effects. They are a form of propaganda.

Propaganda uses information to convince a reader. It uses ideas, facts, or accusations to help or hurt a cause. Because it tries to promote a single point of view, it is generally one-sided. Propaganda often distorts facts. Advertisers use a variety of propaganda techniques to convince us to buy their products. How is this advertiser trying to convince you to buy the product?

---

**TRAIN YOUR VOICE FOR SUCCESS!**

Never again will you be overanxious or fearful when meeting new people or speaking in public. You will be absolutely self-confident knowing that your voice can have the resonance of a Richard Burton, the controlled charm of a Bette Davis, the poise of a Ronald Reagan, or the seductive power of a Julio Iglesias!

Order Your Voice-Training Cassette Right Away!

---

▶ This ad tries to convince you to buy the cassette by claiming that

**(1)** it can make you speak as well as some famous people
**(2)** you can become a famous actor if you use it
**(3)** most people you know have benefited from it already
**(4)** people who use it get better jobs
**(5)** you don't need to improve your public speaking skills

The correct answer is choice (1). This is an example of a very common propaganda technique, the "famous or respected person" technique. By using the names of famous people, the ad tries to get you to think that you'll learn the same techniques that have made these people so successful.

Other common propaganda techniques include:

- Glittering generalities—using vague positive words and images

  Our salon's *secret techniques* will bring out the *timeless beauty* in you. Our experts think *age and elegance* go hand in hand.

- Name calling—connecting a negative image to an idea, a product, a person, or a group

  Stop using *dirty, smelly, smoky* oil. Change to electric heat.

- Bandwagon—everybody is doing it

  Join the Pepsi *Generation*! Drink Pepsi Cola.

- Cardstacking—mentioning only the favorable facts and ignoring the negative facts

  Top Choice Chewing Tobacco gives you that *real tobacco flavor without smoke*. For real tobacco satisfaction, use Top Choice.

  (Not mentioned in the ad are the dangers of smokeless tobacco.)

## EXERCISE 8: PROPAGANDA AND ADVERTISING

*Directions:* Answer the questions following each advertisement.

Drink Budweiser, America's highest-quality beer.
Only the finest barley and hops are used in brewing.

1. According to the ad, you should drink Budweiser because

   **(1)** everybody drinks Budweiser
   **(2)** famous people drink Budweiser
   **(3)** drinking Budweiser will make you popular
   **(4)** more people use Budweiser than any other beer
   **(5)** other breweries use lower-quality barley and hops

2. The ad gives only reasons why you *should* drink Budweiser. Can you think of a reason not to drink Budweiser?_____

_____

Only those who dare . . . truly live
DRIVE A FERRARI

**3.** This ad would appeal to

**(1)** young children who like to play with Cabbage Patch Kids
**(2)** large families looking for a good family car
**(3)** someone who wanted to appear adventurous
**(4)** a banker trying to establish a solid, respectable image
**(5)** a struggling young couple looking for their first car

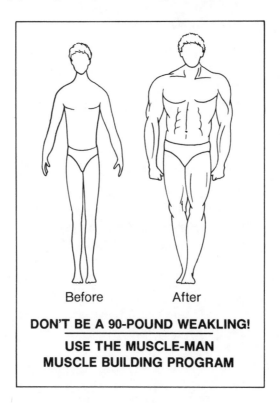

Before          After

**DON'T BE A 90-POUND WEAKLING!**

**USE THE MUSCLE-MAN
MUSCLE BUILDING PROGRAM**

**4.** This ad appeals to people who believe that

**(1)** attractive men have large muscles
**(2)** it is a good idea to keep your weight down
**(3)** it is important to be healthy
**(4)** women like intelligent men
**(5)** it is important to be considerate of others

**5.** Women will be attracted to this ad because

   **(1)** they look like the woman in the drawing
   **(2)** they are tired of the summer and want to look ahead to fall
   **(3)** they are looking for a bargain
   **(4)** they want to think of themselves as sophisticated
   **(5)** they do not want to attract attention to themselves

COME TO LESLIE'S!

We have sophisticated styles for fall.

**Answers start on page 209.**

# Political Propaganda

Propaganda has been used frequently in the political world. A lot of political propaganda consists of advertisements for political candidates. In addition, governments and political candidates use propaganda to convince people to support a cause. Political propaganda is also used to turn public opinion against other people or other countries, as in the following example.

> Englishmen cannot understand great ideas; they lack any real intelligence. They only care about material things and comforts.

▶ These ideas are an example of Italian propaganda at the beginning of World War II. What did the Italian government want its people to believe about the English?

   **(1)** The English were a dangerous enemy who must be feared.
   **(2)** The English were evil people who wanted to destroy the world.
   **(3)** The English were small-minded and could be defeated easily.
   **(4)** The English had a powerful economy that had to be destroyed.
   **(5)** The English were a noble people who should be copied.

The correct answer is choice (3). The writer says that the English lacked real intelligence. The Italian government insulted the English so that the Italian people would be more supportive of the war against the English.

## EXERCISE 9: POLITICAL PROPAGANDA

*Directions:* Answer the questions following each passage or illustration.

Following a disastrous defeat of the Germans by the Soviets at Stalingrad, Goebbels, Hitler's propaganda chief, spoke to the German people. He said that the 300,000 Germans killed in the battle were all heroes. They had slowed down six Soviet armies, which otherwise would be rampaging toward Germany. He claimed that the Germans had been "purified" by the defeat at Stalingrad. It had given them the new strength they required for victory.

**1.** List two reasons that, according to Goebbels, the defeat at Stalingrad was good for the Germans.

_____

_____

**2.** Why would Goebbels have described the terrible outcome of the Battle of Stalingrad as he did?

**(1)** He believed that military defeats were good for the German spirit.
**(2)** He thought the Russians might retreat.
**(3)** He wanted the Americans and British to break their alliance with the USSR.
**(4)** He didn't want people to realize what a disaster it was.
**(5)** He wanted Germany to surrender to the Russians.

### HART MAKES HIS MOVE!!

Recent Poll Shows Gain of Twenty-Three Percentage Points
NOW IS THE TIME TO JOIN THE HART BANDWAGON!

**3.** According to this political advertisement, why should you support Hart?

**(1)** He has the best new ideas.
**(2)** Everybody else is starting to support him.
**(3)** He is the candidate who is best for the country.
**(4)** He has the support of important elected officials.
**(5)** He has the political skills needed to be successful.

In English, this poster says "Benito Mussolini loves children very much. The children of Italy love the Duce very much. Long live the Duce. I salute the Duce: To us!"

**4.** This poster implies that the Italian people should support Mussolini because

    **(1)** he is a great military leader
    **(2)** he has lived a long time
    **(3)** everybody in Italy is related to him
    **(4)** he is a beloved father figure
    **(5)** the enemies of Italy want him defeated

**Answers start on page 209.**

## EXERCISE 10: CHAPTER REVIEW

*Directions:* Study each passage or picture, then answer the questions that follow.

1. This advertisement is trying to convince you that you should use Sauce Royale because

    **(1)** it is the best-tasting sauce
    **(2)** it is the healthiest sauce
    **(3)** it was made for a king
    **(4)** it was made by a famous chef
    **(5)** it is cheaper than other sauces

Questions 2–3 are based on the following map.

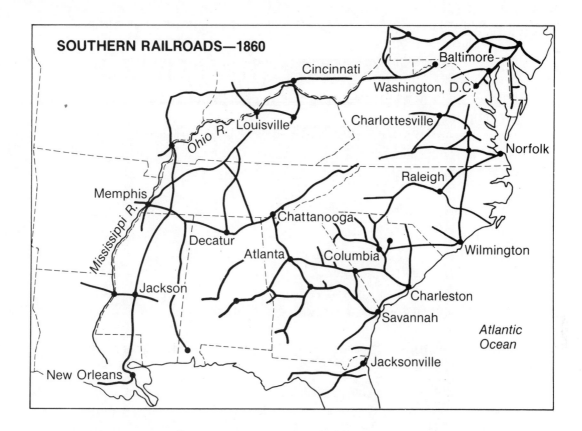

2. According to the map, in 1860 it was impossible to travel by train from

    **(1)** Jackson to New Orleans
    **(2)** Atlanta to Columbia
    **(3)** Atlanta to Chattanooga
    **(4)** Raleigh to Charlottesville
    **(5)** Jacksonville to Savannah

3. There is enough information on the map to determine that

    **(1)** the North would win the Civil War
    **(2)** Atlanta was the largest city in the South
    **(3)** Savannah was the main shipping port for cotton
    **(4)** the western frontier could not be reached from the South by train
    **(5)** the South was mostly farmland

Questions 4–5 are based on the following passage.

Amnesty International is a very special organization. It does not support any one form of government or economic system. It does watch out for human rights throughout the world, working on thousands of cases of political imprisonment, torture, and murder. As a result of this work, many people put into prison or tortured for their beliefs have been freed. Governments have been pressured to end their abuse of people who disagree with them. In recognition of its work, Amnesty International was awarded the Nobel Peace Prize.

**4.** Amnesty International's purpose is

  **(1)** the defeat of communism
  **(2)** the protection of human rights
  **(3)** the growth of democracy
  **(4)** the winning of major awards
  **(5)** the raising of money through contributions

**5.** To decide if Amnesty International has been effective, you would want to know

  **(1)** how many awards it has won
  **(2)** whether it has the support of the United States government
  **(3)** if it has helped make governments more respectful of human rights
  **(4)** whether it has helped in the fight against communism
  **(5)** whether it has been able to raise more money than other human rights groups

Questions 6–7 are based on the following passage.

The United Nations was founded after World War II to help nations solve their differences peacefully. While there has not been another world war, the past forty years have been far from peaceful. For example, in the 1950s, the United Nations sent troops to fight in the Korean War. In addition, there has been almost constant war in Southeast Asia for over half a century. And, even though the United Nations has sent peacekeeping forces to the Middle East, war has raged there for years.

Both the Security Council and the General Assembly of the United Nations were supposed to be places where nations could talk about their differences and solve them without violence. Unfortunately, nations have used these forums to attack each other verbally rather than to settle disputes.

**6.** From the passage, it is clear that

**(1)** the United Nations has failed and should be abolished
**(2)** the United Nations should be given more money
**(3)** the United Nations has promoted war rather than prevented it
**(4)** the United Nations still needs to develop ways to solve disputes peacefully
**(5)** the United Nations should follow American foreign policy

**7.** A guiding principle of the United Nations is

**(1)** only the strong survive
**(2)** the meek shall inherit the earth
**(3)** if you have the votes, you have the power
**(4)** people should be free to live as they choose
**(5)** conflicts should be settled peacefully

**Background clues:** On the July 4th weekend in 1986, there was a huge celebration of the 100th anniversary of the Statue of Liberty.

'OK, FIREBOATS—ON MY SIGNAL, WET THE T-SHIRT!'

**8.** According to the cartoonist, the celebration emphasized

**(1)** the value of liberty
**(2)** the dignity of the American people
**(3)** tasteless commercialism
**(4)** the importance of historical statues
**(5)** the importance of immigrants to our country

**KEEP AMERICA STRONG!**

VOTE FOR VITO AMORELLI FOR U.S. CONGRESS

9. As a voter, what reasonable response might you make to this ad?

   **(1)** voting for Vito because you want America to be strong
   **(2)** voting against Vito because you want America to be weak
   **(3)** not voting at all because it does not matter who is elected
   **(4)** finding out how Vito proposes to keep America strong
   **(5)** running for Congress yourself

10. "Equal pay for equal work" has become a rallying cry for women's groups. On the average, women are paid only two-thirds of what a man receives for either the same job or a job of equal difficulty and responsibility. What might be a good reason for a particular man to be paid more than a particular woman for a similar job?

    **(1)** He needs to be paid more because he must support a family.
    **(2)** Men are more important than women.
    **(3)** He has more years of experience than the woman.
    **(4)** He must save for retirement.
    **(5)** His pride would be hurt if a woman made as much as he.

11. Bill needs to buy a new pair of work gloves. He has to decide whether to buy the Powergrip brand or the Workingman brand. Which of the following is a good reason to buy the Powergrip brand glove?

    **(1)** It is a more durable and comfortable glove.
    **(2)** Robert Redford endorsed Powergrip gloves.
    **(3)** More people buy Powergrip than Workingman.
    **(4)** Bill's neighbor works for the company that makes Powergrip gloves.
    **(5)** Powergrip gloves cost more than Workingman gloves.

**Answers start on page 210.**

## CHAPTER REVIEW EVALUATION CHART

| Reading Skill | Question Numbers* | Review Pages | Number Correct |
|---|---|---|---|
| Enough Information | **2, 3** | 142–145 | _____ /2 |
| Using Relevant Information | 5, 6 | 146–149 | _____ /2 |
| Errors in Reasoning | 10, 11 | 149–153 | _____ /2 |
| Recognizing Values | 4, 7, **8** | 154–157 | _____ /3 |
| Propaganda | **1**, 9 | 158–163 | _____ /2 |

*Question numbers in **dark type** are based on illustrations.

Your score: _____ out of 11

Passing score: 8 out of 11

# 6
# Applying Information in Social Studies

Your mother just had a heart attack and has been rushed to the hospital in a city over a thousand miles from where you live. You want to get there as soon as possible so that you can be with her. What form of transportation would you take?

You would probably go by airplane rather than by car, bus, or train. And you wouldn't even consider riding a bicycle or walking. By deciding to take a plane, you would be applying your knowledge of different types of transportation to your own needs.

## WHAT IS APPLICATION?

Every day, you put the skills and information you have learned in your life to work for you in different situations. In this chapter, you will be applying information in a passage to new situations, just as you applied your knowledge of transportation to the situation described above. You will also study practical applications of information on maps, charts, and graphs, such as using information on a road map.

# Applying Information in Everyday Life

Often you read or hear information you can apply to your daily needs. You are always picking up information and using it. For example, what do you think you might do to protect yourself or others if you read the following article in your daily newspaper?

### Tylenol Tragedy

Police reported that five people in the Chicago area have died from taking Tylenol capsules laced with cyanide. Authorities say that the killer opened the capsules and added the cyanide. The bottles were then resealed and placed on store shelves. At this time the police have no suspects.

▶ What would you do? _____

_____

You might have done several things. First, you would probably throw away any Tylenol capsules you had. You also wouldn't buy any more until you were sure the capsules were safe. You also might think of warning other people, especially your family, of the danger of taking Tylenol capsules.

By responding to the article, you would have applied the information that Tylenol capsules are dangerous. In the following exercise, you'll practice this skill.

## EXERCISE 1: APPLYING INFORMATION IN EVERYDAY LIFE

*Directions:* Read each passage, then choose the correct answer for each question that follows.

Regular exercise is more effective than dieting in helping people lose weight. A recent survey found that people who exercised for at least fifteen minutes at least three times per week were able to lose more weight than people using popular weight-loss diets. In a follow-up survey of the same people six months later, most exercisers had maintained their weight loss, while almost half the dieters had already regained what they had lost.

1. Earl wants to lose twenty pounds. Based on the information in the passage, what would be the best way for him to lose the weight and keep it off?

   (1) take diet pills and consume fewer calories
   (2) skip lunch every day
   (3) try the Scarsdale diet
   (4) play tennis or basketball every weekend
   (5) walk briskly three miles at least three times a week

Automation has transformed the modern office. Word processors are rapidly taking over most of the functions of a typewriter, and copy machines and computer printers have replaced carbon paper. Many executives use tape recorders instead of dictating to a secretary who takes shorthand. In addition, large amounts of information are stored in computer databases instead of in file cabinets, and spreadsheet computer programs are replacing bookkeeper's ledgers. Offices can even send information from their computers to computers in other offices through electronic mail. With all these changes, in the next few years employers' greatest need will be people trained to use this new equipment.

2. Karl, who wants to find work in an office, read the previous passage in a brochure on career opportunities. Based on the passage, to help him find and keep a job, he should

   (1) learn to repair electronic equipment
   (2) take a course in shorthand, since stenographers are becoming very rare
   (3) work hard to increase his typing speed
   (4) get training in computer use in business offices
   (5) buy a newspaper and apply for jobs that sound interesting

**Answers start on page 210.**

# Applying Information in a Passage

In social studies, you are often asked to apply information you read in a passage to answer a question or solve a problem. In the following example, you have a passage to read and then some choices to make. Apply the information in the passage to help you make the choices.

One hundred fifty years ago, farmers had to make the most of what they had. Typical farm families grew their own food. They also had a variety of farm animals, perhaps including cows, horses, pigs, and sheep. Their everyday clothes might be made from materials grown on the farm, such as wool, leather, cotton, and other fibers. Their homes were made from materials they could gather—wood, stones, even earth.

However, a farm family could not provide for all its needs. Plows, tools, nails, and other metal items were made by a blacksmith. Bowls and plates were made by a potter or imported. Glass windows, storage barrels, and wagon wheels were other items that a farmer had to purchase.

Put a *P* in front of those items that a farm family could *produce* on its farm. Put a *B* in front of those items that a farm family had to *buy*.

_____ **1.** wooden spoons

_____ **2.** milk

_____ **3.** horseshoes

_____ **4.** corn

_____ **5.** tin lantern

You should have put a *P* in front of 1, 2, and 4. The farm family could carve wooden spoons, get milk from its own cow, and grow corn. You should have put a *B* in front of 3 and 5, horseshoes and a tin lantern. These would have to be bought from someone who could work metal.

## EXERCISE 2: APPLYING INFORMATION IN A PASSAGE

*Directions:* Read each passage carefully, then answer the questions that follow.

A variety of government agencies provide services to people who need help. The Department of Human Services provides welfare benefits, including Aid to Families with Dependent Children and food stamps. The Rehabilitation Commission helps handicapped people get the special programs and services they need. The Council on Aging is an agency that provides elderly people with a variety of resources.

Following are descriptions of some people and the type of assistance they need. In the blank, mark the agency each should go to for help—*H* for Department of Human Services, *R* for the Rehabilitation Commission, and *A* for the Council on Aging.

_____ **1.** A woman with two small children has been abandoned by her husband and has no job.

_____ **2.** A seventy-one-year-old woman is lonely and wants to get out and spend time with other people.

_____ **3.** A deaf man wants training in order to work with computers.

_____ **4.** A family of four does not have enough money to buy food.

The development of the American West is limited by a shortage of water. Farmers, industry, residents, and recreational facilities all compete for water. In the future, communities will have to decide how to use their limited water supply. Will they use their water to grow more crops, to run more factories, to provide for a larger population and more homes, or to expand resorts and recreational facilities?

The city of Kerr has decided that its water will be put to best use for new homes and recreational development. The city is attractive to retired people as well as to tourists. The city council feels that construction of new homes, parks, and resorts will keep Kerr's economy strong.

Under this policy, which of the following requests for water access should the city approve? Write *yes* next to the projects the city *should* approve under the policy. Write *no* next to the projects the city should *not* approve.

_____ 5. An oil company wants to build a processing plant near Kerr and wants access to the city's water supply.

_____ 6. St. Mary's Hospital wants to build a new, larger facility to better meet the needs of the growing elderly population.

_____ 7. A chain of amusement parks wants to build a theme park outside Kerr and wants access to the city's water supply.

_____ 8. A farmer wants to buy a large piece of unirrigated land next to his farm. He wants permission to extend his watering system to the unirrigated land.

**Answers start on page 210.**

# Applying Information on a Map

You can apply the information contained on all kinds of maps to real situations and decisions. Maps that you might come across in your everyday life include road maps, subway maps, and weather maps.

One of the most common ways that you might use a map is for deciding how to get from one place to another. For example, when you are trying to figure out a driving route, you look for the most direct route, the one that is closest to a straight line between the two places.

▶ You are a resident of Denver, Colorado. You want to drive to Los Angeles. Based on the interstate map on the next page, describe the shortest route you should take. _____

First find Denver and Los Angeles on the map. Then find the route that is closest to a straight line. You should have taken Route 70 west to Route 15 south to Route 10 west.

**INTERSTATE ROAD MAP—WESTERN UNITED STATES**

# EXERCISE 3: APPLYING MAP SKILLS

*Directions:* Use information from the maps to answer the following questions. Questions 1–2 are based on the interstate road map above.

1. You live in Olympia, Washington, and want to visit your brother in Cheyenne, Wyoming. What is the most direct route you could take?

   _____

   _____

2. You live in San Diego and want to travel to El Paso to see a rodeo. What is the shortest route you could take? _____

   _____

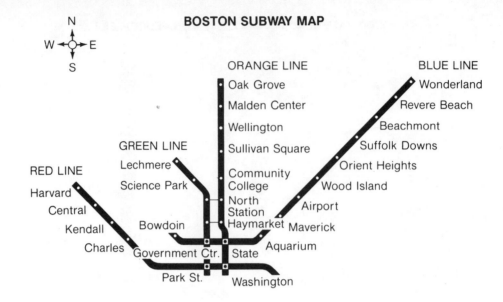

BOSTON SUBWAY MAP

**3.** How do you get from the airport to North Station on the Boston subway?

**(1)** Take the Orange Line south to State and change to the Blue Line.
**(2)** Take the Blue Line southwest to State and change to the Red Line going northwest.
**(3)** Take the Orange Line south to Washington and change to the Blue Line going northwest.
**(4)** Take the Blue Line southwest to State and change to the Orange Line going north.
**(5)** Take the Blue Line southwest.

**4.** A student at Harvard University wants to visit the Science Museum at Science Park. How would she get there by subway?

**(1)** Take the Red Line southeast.
**(2)** Take the Green Line north.
**(3)** Take the Red Line southeast to Park St. and change to the Green Line going north.
**(4)** Take the Blue Line southwest to Government Center and change to the Green Line going north.
**(5)** Take the Red Line southeast to Park St. and change to the Orange Line going north.

**Answers start on page 210.**

# Applying Data on Charts and Graphs

In social studies, you will often be asked to apply the information on charts and graphs when you need to solve a problem. In the following example, apply the information on the bar graph to figure out what the board of education's long-range plan should be. The Mozlin Board of Education is planning ahead three years for its high school building and teachers.

**STUDENT POPULATION, MOZLIN PUBLIC SCHOOLS**

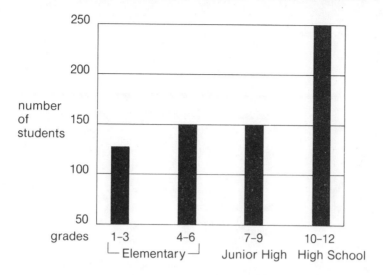

1.  How many students are there now in grades 10–12? _____

2.  How many students are there now in grades 7–9? _____

3.  In three years, will the student body of the Mozlin High School have increased, decreased, or remained about the same? _____

4.  Given the information on the bar graph, which of the following should the board of education plan to do within three years?

    **(1)** hire more high school teachers
    **(2)** build a second high school
    **(3)** close the high school, because there won't be any students
    **(4)** reduce the number of high school teachers
    **(5)** send overflow students to other schools

1. There are 250 students. Find grades 10–12 on the horizontal axis. Go to the top of the bar above 10–12 and read the number of students from the vertical axis.

2. There are 150 students. Find grades 7–9 on the horizontal axis and read the height of the bar.

3. The student body in the high school will decrease. Compare the top of the 7–9 bar with the top of the 10–12 bar. In three years the current junior high students (7–9) will be in high school. That means that in three years there will be about 150 students in the high school, many fewer than the 250 there now.

4. The correct answer is choice (4), *reduce the number of high school teachers*. Since there will be fewer students, fewer teachers will be needed. Choices (1), (2), and (5) are incorrect because there will be fewer students. The school should not close, choice (3), since there will still be students.

## EXERCISE 4: APPLYING INFORMATION ON CHARTS AND GRAPHS

*Directions:* Use the information from each chart or graph to answer the questions.

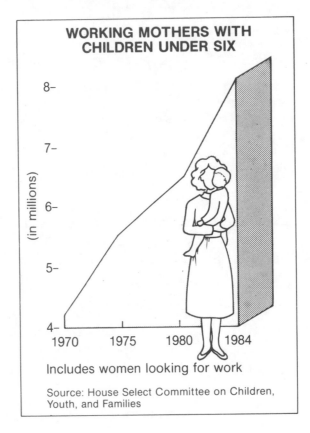

**WORKING MOTHERS WITH CHILDREN UNDER SIX**

Includes women looking for work

Source: House Select Committee on Children, Youth, and Families

1. What change does the graph show taking place between 1970 and 1984?

   **(1)** More women with children under six years of age decided to stay home.
   **(2)** There are fewer women with children under six.
   **(3)** The number of working mothers with children under six has almost doubled.
   **(4)** Working mothers have learned more about health care for children under six.
   **(5)** The number of working mothers with children under six has stabilized.

2. Based on this information, a new company that wanted to attract young women into its work force might consider offering

   **(1)** security guards at night in areas where women work
   **(2)** Club Med vacations
   **(3)** on-site day-care facilities
   **(4)** on-site athletic facilities
   **(5)** weekly social events in the evenings

| CONSUMER REPORTER TELEPHONE COMPARISON | | | |
|---|---|---|---|
| **Phone** | **Price** | **Durability** | **Ease of Use** |
| Sunbrand SlimPhone | $55 | excellent | poor |
| Blackdeck Desktop | $75 | good | excellent |
| Radio House Cordless | $85 | fair | poor |
| HomePhone Basic | $25 | fair | good |

**3.** Mary is buying a phone for her elderly father, whose hands are stiffened by arthritis. Which phone should she choose?

_____

**4.** Leonard is buying a phone for the kitchen in his home. The phone will be in constant use by his family of six, including his four teenaged children. Which phone should he choose?

_____

**5.** Lydia has just moved out of her parents' home. She has only a few hundred dollars saved to furnish her apartment. Her job requires that she have a phone at home. Which phone should she choose?

_____

**Answers start on page 211.**

## EXERCISE 5: CHAPTER REVIEW

*Directions:* Answer the questions following each passage or illustration.

Questions 1–2 are based on the following map.

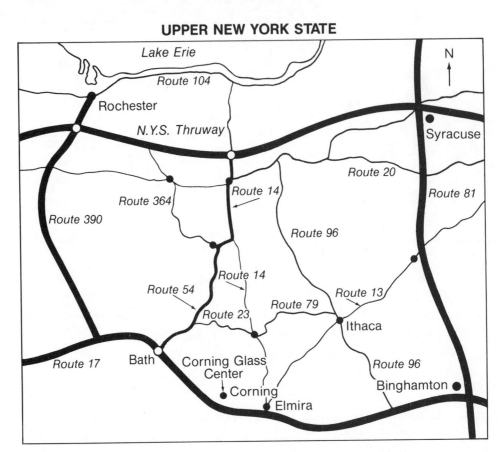

**UPPER NEW YORK STATE**

1. You live in Rochester and want to visit the Corning Glass Center in Corning. What is the most direct route you could take?

   **(1)** Route 390 south to NYS Thruway east to Route 14 south to Route 17 west
   **(2)** Route 390 south to NYS Thruway east to Route 14 south to Route 54 south to Route 17 east
   **(3)** Route 104 east to Route 14 south to Route 17 west
   **(4)** Route 390 south to NYS Thruway east to Route 81 south to Route 17 west
   **(5)** Route 390 south to Route 17 east

2. The shortest route from the city of Syracuse to the town of Bath is

   **(1)** NYS Thruway west to Route 14 south to Route 17 west
   **(2)** NYS Thruway west to Route 14 south to Route 54 south
   **(3)** NYS Thruway west to Route 390 south to Route 17 east
   **(4)** Route 81 south to Route 17 west
   **(5)** Route 81 south to Route 13 south to Route 17 west

Questions 3–4 are based on the following chart.

| COMPACT CAR COMPARISON CHART | | | |
|---|---|---|---|
| | **Price** | **Gas Mileage** | **Repair Record** |
| Ford Flicker | $5500 | 25 city 30 highway | poor |
| Chevrolet Pony | $5600 | 27 city 32 highway | better than average |
| Dodge Rainbow | $6100 | 30 city 38 highway | better than average |
| AMC Miniko | $6500 | 23 city 30 highway | average |
| Chrysler Prince | $6600 | 28 city 33 highway | average |

3. Mario is a traveling salesman in a rural area. He drives mostly on highways and needs a very reliable car. Which car from the chart above should he buy?

   **(1)** Ford Flicker
   **(2)** Chevrolet Pony
   **(3)** Dodge Rainbow
   **(4)** AMC Miniko
   **(5)** Chrysler Prince

4. Libby cannot afford to pay more than $5800 for a car. She also wants to buy a car that will have low repair costs. Which car from the chart above should she buy?

   **(1)** Ford Flicker
   **(2)** Chevrolet Pony
   **(3)** Dodge Rainbow
   **(4)** AMC Miniko
   **(5)** Chrysler Prince

Question 5 is based on the following paragraph.

In order to ensure a stable food supply for the United States, the U.S. government has an extensive farm support program. This program pays farmers not to plant some of their fields, since we don't need the food right now. These fields are not given up for other uses because they could be needed to produce food in the future. These idle fields could be planted to respond to a national food emergency, such as failure of an important crop because of major drought or disease.

**5.** Based on the passage, the federal government should *not* pay farmers to preserve unplanted tobacco fields because

   **(1)** tobacco farmers do not practice sound farm management
   **(2)** enough tobacco is being produced
   **(3)** cigarettes have been shown to cause cancer
   **(4)** tobacco would not be needed in a national food emergency
   **(5)** the tobacco lobby in Washington has been weakened by antismoking campaigns

Questions 6–7 are based on the following passage.

Teenagers today seem angry, and they lack direction. They often express their frustrations through antisocial, even violent, acts such as breaking windows, spray painting profanity on walls, or stealing cars. Poor children are not the only ones who commit these crimes. These things happen in wealthy suburbs as well.

Because rich teens get in trouble just as deprived teens do, we cannot blame their crimes on their not having money or possessions they want. Instead, we must realize that these young people have almost nothing useful or important to do. They have a lot of energy to use up. If they have no positive outlet for their energy, it will come out in a destructive way.

**6.** The author of this passage feels that teenagers commit crimes because

   **(1)** they want money
   **(2)** they don't have their own cars
   **(3)** they have nothing useful to do
   **(4)** they have no outlet for their artistic urges
   **(5)** they don't know any better

**7.** Based on the author's theory, which of the following would be a successful way of fighting teen crime?

(1) raising the drinking age
(2) giving kids more money to spend
(3) providing kids with free spray paint
(4) increasing penalties for juvenile crimes
(5) having young people do community service work

**Answers start on page 211.**

## CHAPTER 6 REVIEW EVALUATION CHART

| Reading Skill | Question Numbers* | Review Pages | Number Correct |
|---|---|---|---|
| Application— reading passages | 5, 6, 7 | 170–174 | _____ /3 |
| Application— maps | **1, 2** | 174–176 | _____ /2 |
| Application— charts & graphs | **3, 4** | 176–179 | _____ /2 |

*Question numbers in **dark type** are based on illustrations.

Your score: _____ out of 7

Passing score: 5 out of 7

# Posttest

The posttest should give you a good idea of how well you have learned the skills you have studied in this book. You should take the posttest after you have completed all the chapters.

*Directions:* Study each passage or illustration, then answer the questions that follow.

Questions 1–2 are based on the following passage.

> That man over there says that woman needs to be helped into carriages and lifted over ditches. . . . Nobody ever helps me into carriages, or over mud-puddles, or gives me any best place. And a'nt I a woman?
>
> Look at my arm! I have ploughed, and planted, and gathered into barns, and no man could head me! And a'nt I a woman?
>
> I would work as much and eat as much as a man, when I could get it, and bear the lash as well. And a'nt I a woman?
>
> I have borne thirteen children and seen 'em most all sold off to slavery, and when I cried out with my mother's grief, none but Jesus heard me! And a'nt I a woman?

1. Who is the speaker in this passage?

   (1) a modern politician running for office
   (2) a black woman who was a slave
   (3) a wealthy, nineteenth-century southern woman
   (4) an early settler in New England
   (5) a twentieth-century feminist

**2.** When the speaker in this passage says, "Look at my arm! I have ploughed, and planted, and gathered into barns, and no man could head me!" she means that

(1) she could work as hard as any man
(2) she was forced to do work that women shouldn't have to do
(3) she loved farming
(4) she appreciates the help that men have given her
(5) in order to be a real woman, one must do hard physical labor

Questions 3–5 are based on the following passage.

Neither Larry Bird nor Wayne Gretzky has a reputation as a mental giant. When Bird was seen reading a book, his teammates were stunned. Gretzky, who never finished high school, prefers casino gambling and the soap opera "The Young and the Restless" to reading.

Yet Bird, the National Basketball Association's Most Valuable Player for three straight seasons, and Gretzky, the National Hockey League's leading scorer for the last five seasons, excel at sports for reasons that go far beyond speed and physical skill. They also possess an uncanny ability to stay several moves ahead of the other players. They always know exactly what has just happened. They also know what will happen in the next few seconds.

Bird's and Gretzky's special talents would not show up on ordinary intelligence tests. However, these men would rank high in intelligence according to a new theory proposed by psychologist Howard Gardner. Gardner says that people have seven different types of intelligence, one of which is the physical intelligence of athletes and dancers. Judged by Gardner's standard, Bird and Gretzky would probably be classed as geniuses.

**3.** Something that Larry Bird and Wayne Gretzky have in common is that they

(1) are considered geniuses by accepted standards
(2) enjoy similar ways of relaxing, including casino gambling and soap operas
(3) are able to stay several moves ahead of other players in a game
(4) are interested in exploring new theories of intelligence
(5) have worked with psychologist Howard Gardner

4. Since Bird and Gretzky would rank very high in physical intelligence, you could conclude that

   **(1)** most professional athletes are geniuses
   **(2)** football star quarterback Dan Marino would also rank high in physical intelligence
   **(3)** they would be geniuses on conventional intelligence scales
   **(4)** they are two of the most intelligent people in the world
   **(5)** Woody Allen, a talented film director and comedian, would also rank high in physical intelligence

5. Gardner's theory of intelligence says that

   **(1)** athletes are smarter than most people
   **(2)** hockey and basketball players are the smartest athletes
   **(3)** ordinary intelligence tests measure physical intelligence
   **(4)** only one kind of intelligence can be measured
   **(5)** people have seven different types of intelligence

Questions 6–7 are based on the following illustration.

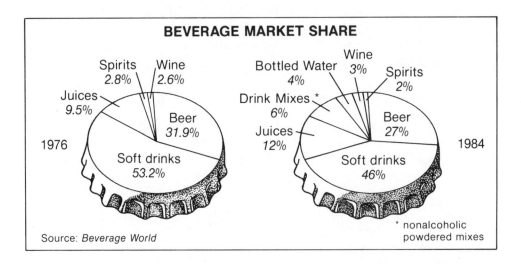

6. Which of the following was a new factor in the drink market in 1984?

   **(1)** juices
   **(2)** soft drinks
   **(3)** beer
   **(4)** bottled water
   **(5)** wine

**7.** From 1976 to 1984, which type of beverage suffered the greatest loss of market share?

   **(1)** beer
   **(2)** bottled water
   **(3)** drink mixes
   **(4)** juices
   **(5)** soft drinks

Question 8 is based on the following passage.

> "I can't make a damn thing out of this tax problem," complained President Warren G. Harding to a friend. "I listen to one side and they seem right and then—God!—I talk to the other side and they seem to be right. . . . I know that somewhere there is a book that will give me the truth, but I couldn't read the book. I know somewhere there is an economist who knows the truth, but I don't know where to find him and haven't the sense to know him and trust him when I find him. God! What a job."

**8.** The main idea of this paragraph is that Warren G. Harding

   **(1)** provided leadership on the tax issue
   **(2)** did not know what to do about the tax problem
   **(3)** needed to hire a new economist
   **(4)** wanted to read more books about taxes
   **(5)** thought that taxes were not a serious problem

Questions 9–11 are based on the following passage.

> The days of the station wagon and the big families going to drive-in movies are just about over. Drive-in movie theatres that are still open have managed to survive by showing X-rated films.
>
> Drive-ins are dying for one simple reason—people don't go to them anymore. Box office sales have suffered from the popularity of VCRs and theatres in shopping malls.
>
> Drive-in owners are also tempted to sell to land-hungry developers, who are willing to pay big bucks for property near major highways. One by one, the drive-ins are being replaced by shopping centers and industrial parks.

**9.** Drive-ins are losing customers because

   **(1)** land has become more expensive
   **(2)** people have smaller families than they used to
   **(3)** VCRs and mall theatres are taking away business
   **(4)** there are fewer X-rated films
   **(5)** industrial parks are being built on their former sites

**10.** The main idea of this passage is that

    **(1)** the days of the drive-in are just about over
    **(2)** drive-ins will survive by showing X-rated movies
    **(3)** drive-ins cannot compete with VCRs and mall theatres
    **(4)** drive-ins are being bought up by land-hungry developers
    **(5)** drive-ins are an important part of American life

**11.** Given the information in this passage, you might predict that in ten years

    **(1)** drive-ins will make a strong comeback
    **(2)** land prices will go down
    **(3)** automakers will stop making station wagons
    **(4)** many existing drive-ins will be closed
    **(5)** there will be more X-rated films

Questions 12–13 are based on the following chart.

| U.S. PETROLEUM IMPORTS BY SOURCE (thousands of barrels per day) | | | | | |
| --- | --- | --- | --- | --- | --- |
| Source | 1978 | 1979 | 1980 | 1981 | 1982 |
| Arab OPEC | 2,963 | 3,056 | 2,551 | 1,848 | 840 |
| Other OPEC | 2,788 | 2,581 | 1,749 | 1,475 | 1,273 |
| Non-OPEC | 2,613 | 2,819 | 2,609 | 2,672 | 2,928 |
| Total | 8,364 | 8,456 | 6,909 | 5,995 | 5,041 |

**12.** American oil imports peaked in the year

    **(1)** 1978
    **(2)** 1979
    **(3)** 1980
    **(4)** 1981
    **(5)** 1982

**13.** Based on this chart, you could conclude that between 1979 and 1982

    **(1)** imported oil from Arab OPEC members dropped dramatically
    **(2)** Americans increased their dependence on foreign oil
    **(3)** OPEC expanded its influence in the United States
    **(4)** United States demand for oil remained steady
    **(5)** Americans ended their dependence on foreign oil

Questions 14–15 are based on the following illustration.

**Background Clues:**   Gorbachev, the leader of the USSR, has worked hard to improve his country's image in the world. He has met with President Reagan, made new arms control proposals, paid a seventy-year-old debt to Britain, and allowed a Soviet soccer team to play games outside the Soviet bloc.

MR. WONDERFUL

**14.** The part of this cartoon that is the key to understanding it is Gorbachev's

  **(1)** old-fashioned hat
  **(2)** teeth
  **(3)** business suit
  **(4)** necktie
  **(5)** closed eyes

**15.** The opinion of the cartoonist is that

  **(1)** dentistry has advanced in the USSR
  **(2)** it is important to be well dressed
  **(3)** we must beware of Mr. Gorbachev
  **(4)** Gorbachev can be trusted
  **(5)** we must reach an arms agreement with the USSR

Questions 16–18 are based on the following passage.

Sociologist David Riesman, in his book *The Lonely Crowd*, describes two types of Americans. First, there is the inner-directed person whose life is controlled by his or her own strongly held inner values. An example of an inner-directed man is the rugged frontierman, who has to rely on himself while he works on his homestead.

The second type of American is other-directed. Other-directed people are more interested in the approval of other people than in values. A member of a teenage gang and a successful mid-level manager in a large company are examples of other-directed people.

16. Which ad might appeal to an inner-directed man?

(1) A lone, good-looking cowboy on a horse is lighting a cigarette. The ad reads, "This is Marlboro country."
(2) "Subaru is the largest-selling car in New England."
(3) "Come join millions! Celebrate the 100th anniversary of the Statue of Liberty in New York."
(4) "Come to Disney World, the dream vacation for every child!"
(5) "Buy Crest, America's best-selling toothpaste."

17. An other-directed person generally

(1) is a gang member
(2) needs the approval of others
(3) likes to be in the wilderness
(4) is an independent thinker
(5) works as a manager

18. An example of an other-directed person is

(1) an independent, millionaire oilman
(2) a bad-tempered, foul-mouthed tennis star
(3) a nun who leaves the church because she can no longer follow its teachings
(4) a member of a religious sect
(5) a hermit

> **WOMEN!**
> Fight the Equal Rights Amendment!
> It will not help you—It will hurt you.
>
> The Equal Rights Amendment is a threat to all women. If it passes, it will rob you of
>
> - your right to be a homemaker
> - your protection from being drafted and serving in combat
> - your right to alimony

**19.** The writers of the above ad want women to believe that the Equal Rights Amendment will

    **(1)** take privileges away from women
    **(2)** promote male control of society
    **(3)** require that men and women use the same bathrooms
    **(4)** ensure that women dominate society
    **(5)** be fair to both men and women

Questions 20–22 are based on the following passage.

        Over one hundred years ago, Henry David Thoreau went to jail to protest the Mexican War. In recent times, many people have followed Thoreau's example and openly broken a law in order to bring public attention to injustice.

        The great Indian leader Gandhi took Thoreau's ideas further. When convicted of breaking a law, Gandhi would serve a prison sentence rather than pay the smallest fine. In prison, he went on hunger strikes to draw even more attention to himself and his cause, the independence of India from Great Britain.

        When good and caring people are thrown in jail for their beliefs, it often makes others think about the laws and conditions that they are trying to change. Peaceful but determined protesters in the United States, such as Martin Luther King, Jr., were inspired by Gandhi and adapted his ideas to the struggle for racial equality. When King and others were jailed for their beliefs, they helped many Americans realize that segregation was wrong. Their example helped strike down the laws that kept segregation alive.

**20.** According to the passage, Martin Luther King, Jr.,

    **(1)** should have been jailed for breaking the law
    **(2)** was an outlaw and a threat to society
    **(3)** helped change laws through nonviolent protesting
    **(4)** had no respect for justice
    **(5)** was a hero because he solved problems by using force

**21.** After Martin Luther King, Jr., went to jail,

    **(1)** Thoreau was jailed for his beliefs
    **(2)** segregation laws in the United States started changing
    **(3)** India won its independence from Great Britain
    **(4)** Gandhi went on a hunger strike
    **(5)** the United States fought the Mexican War

**22.** It is the author's opinion that

    **(1)** Thoreau opposed the Mexican War
    **(2)** Gandhi went to jail rather than pay fines
    **(3)** Martin Luther King, Jr., used the nonviolent tactics of Gandhi
    **(4)** Gandhi was a great leader
    **(5)** segregation laws are no longer legal in the United States

Questions 23–24 are based on the following map.

**THE WAR IN NORTH AFRICA**

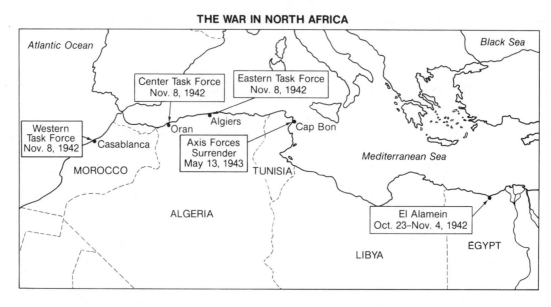

**23.** In what country did the Axis forces in North Africa surrender?

    **(1)** Egypt
    **(2)** Libya
    **(3)** Tunisia
    **(4)** Algeria
    **(5)** Morocco

**24.** How much time elapsed from the first Allied victory in North Africa at El Alamein on November 4, 1942, to the landing of the Western, Center, and Eastern Task Forces at Casablanca, Oran, and Algiers?

    **(1)** 6 months
    **(2)** 3 months
    **(3)** 23 days
    **(4)** 1 week
    **(5)** 4 days

Questions 25–26 are based on the following passage.

> Of all the original thirteen colonies, Pennsylvania attracted the most non-English settlers. It was also the colony that had the greatest tolerance of religious and cultural differences. It had been founded by Quakers, led by William Penn, who wanted to create a colony based on religious freedom and fairness to all people.

**25.** An important value of the founders of Pennsylvania was

   **(1)** economic freedom
   **(2)** keeping different nationalities separate
   **(3)** conversion of the Indians to Christianity
   **(4)** religious freedom
   **(5)** getting back to nature

**26.** A likely reason that Pennsylvania attracted more non-English settlers than any other colony is that

   **(1)** the climate was better than in any other colony
   **(2)** it was the most tolerant of different people's beliefs
   **(3)** English settlers preferred to go elsewhere
   **(4)** it had the best natural resources
   **(5)** it was run by the Quakers, who had a reputation for good management

Questions 27–28 are based on the following passage.

> Americans love talk shows. For years national television shows like "The Tonight Show" and "Donahue" have been very popular and sometimes controversial. But both of them have been pushed aside by a radio talk show, "Sexually Speaking," hosted by Dr. Ruth Westheimer. In her thick German accent, "Doktah Roos" gives out advice on the air to people calling from all over the country. She claims that she does not do therapy, but attempts to educate. In any case, her show is bold, explicit, and enormously popular.

**27.** According to the passage, the name of the host of the most popular talk show is

   **(1)** "Sexually Speaking"
   **(2)** "The Tonight Show"
   **(3)** "Donahue"
   **(4)** Dr. Ruth Westheimer
   **(5)** Johnny Carson

**28.** There is enough information in the passage to determine that

(1) Americans are very interested in sex
(2) Americans prefer radio to television
(3) the popularity of Dr. Ruth Westheimer will be short-lived
(4) Dr. Ruth Westheimer lives in Germany
(5) Dr. Ruth's show is a valuable educational experience

Questions 29–30 are based on the following passage.

When the Canadian armed forces held their largest maneuvers in several decades in Alberta last May and June, they fielded all the tanks they had in the country—a total of 18.

This is fewer than the number Britain and West Germany maintain at their own armored training centers in western Canada, according to Canadian officers.

And as Canadians like to point out, their navy is now outnumbered in submarines by an amusement park at a shopping mall in Edmonton. The park had four submarines built to take customers on underwater rides. The navy has three obsolete diesel subs to patrol over 36,300 miles of coastlines on three oceans.

**29.** According to the passage, the Canadian armed forces

(1) are well prepared for war
(2) don't have enough soldiers to operate their tanks and submarines
(3) don't have many tanks or submarines
(4) are trying to recruit women soldiers
(5) are developing nuclear weapons

**30.** In training centers in western Canada, Britain and West Germany

(1) assist the Canadian armed forces in defending Canada
(2) are preparing to attack the United States
(3) are building more submarines for Canada
(4) refuse to allow their soldiers to visit amusement parks
(5) maintain more than eighteen tanks

# POSTTEST EVALUATION CHART

Use the answer key on pages 196–197 to check your answers. Then, find the number of each question you missed on this chart and circle it in the second column. Then you will know which chapters you might need to review before you move on to Contemporary's GED-level social studies book.

| | Skill | Item Numbers | Number Correct |
|---|---|---|---|
| **Ch. 1** | Finding details | 5, 27 | _____ /8 |
| | Words in context | 17 | |
| | Restating information | 2 | |
| | Summarizing information | 20, 29 | |
| | Main idea of a paragraph | 8 | |
| | Main idea of a passage | 10 | |
| **Ch. 2** | Locating information on a chart | 12 | _____ /4 |
| | Locating information on a graph | 6 | |
| | Interpreting graphs | 7 | |
| | Locating information on a map | 23 | |
| **Ch. 3** | Sequence | 21 | _____ /4 |
| | Sequence on Maps | 24 | |
| | Cause and effect | 9 | |
| | Compare and contrast | 3 | |
| **Ch. 4** | Fact and opinion | 22 | _____ /6 |
| | Inference | 1 | |
| | Political cartoons | 14, 15 | |
| | Hypotheses | 26 | |
| | Predicting outcomes | 11 | |
| **Ch. 5** | Adequacy of information | 28, 30 | _____ /6 |
| | Intepreting charts | 13 | |
| | Logical reasoning | 4 | |
| | Values | 25 | |
| | Propaganda | 19 | |
| **Ch. 6** | Application | 16, 18 | _____ /2 |

## POSTTEST ANSWER KEY

1. (2) The writer says she could "bear the lash," and the last paragraph states that she had borne thirteen children and seen most of them sold as slaves.

2. (1) She describes heavy farm work that she did. When she says that no man could "head" her, she means that no man could do any more work than she.

3. (3) The second paragraph tells you that they both possess an uncanny ability to stay several moves ahead of the other players.

4. (2) Marino is a star athlete just like Bird and Gretsky. It makes sense that he would have high physical intelligence also.

5. (5) The last paragraph tells you that Gardner says that people have seven different types of intelligence.

6. (4) All of the other choices, except for bottled water, appear on the graph for 1976 as well as on the graph for 1984.

7. (5) Among the choices, both beer and soft drinks lost market share. However, soft drinks lost a larger percentage of market share than beer did.

8. (2) The first sentence states the main idea: "I can't make a damn thing out of this tax problem." In the rest of the paragraph, Harding describes his confusion and need for guidance.

9. (3) In the second paragraph, you are told that box office sales have suffered from the popularity of VCRs and theatres in shopping malls.

10. (1) The first sentence states that the days of the station wagon and the big families going to the drive-in are just about over. The rest of the passage paints a bleak future for the remaining drive-ins.

11. (4) The last sentence states that the drive-ins are being replaced by shopping centers and industrial parks. There is no indication that the trend could reverse.

12. (2) The highest number in the "Total" row is 8,456, which is in the 1979 column.

13. (1) Imports from Arab OPEC countries dropped from 3,056,000 barrels a day in 1979 to 840,000 barrels a day in 1982. If you test the other choices against the data on the chart, you can see that none are true.

14. (2) His teeth are drawn to look like missiles, and they look very threatening. In addition, his teeth are the most noticeable part of the drawing.

15. (3) Because of his teeth, Mr. Gorbachev looks very dangerous, in spite of his smile.

16. (1) The lone cowboy looks like a tough, independent individual, an inner-directed person.

17. (2) *Other-directed* is defined in the second paragraph as a person who is more interested in the approval of other people than in values.

18. (4) A devout member of a religious sect would look for approval from others in the sect.

19. (1) The writers of the ad listed some privileges that women might want. The ad says, if the Equal Rights Amendment passes, women will not be able to have these privileges.

20. (3) The last paragraph describes Martin Luther King, Jr., as a peaceful but determined protester. It goes on to say that, when King was jailed for his beliefs, he helped strike down segregation laws.

21. (2) The last sentence states that, after King and others were jailed, the laws began changing.

**22.** (4)  Gandhi did many important things, and many people consider him a great leader. However, this is a personal belief. The other choices are facts that can be proven.

**23.** (3)  According to the map, the Axis forces surrendered on May 13, 1943, at Cap Bon in Tunisia.

**24.** (5)  According to the map, the Western Task Force at Casablanca, the Center Task Force at Oran, and the Eastern Task Force at Algiers all landed on November 8, 1942, just four days after the end of the battle of El Alamein.

**25.** (4)  The passage states that the colony had the greatest tolerance of religious differences and that the Quakers wanted to create a colony based on religious freedom.

**26.** (2)  Since the colony was the most tolerant of other people's beliefs, it makes sense that it would attract people who were different from the English.

**27.** (4)  The passage states that Dr. Ruth Westheimer's show has pushed aside the other very popular talk shows.

**28.** (1)  The fact that a talk show called "Sexually Speaking" is extremely popular is evidence that Americans are very interested in sex.

**29.** (3)  The passage says that Canada has eighteen tanks and three submarines. Britain and West Germany keep more tanks in Canada than Canada does, and an amusement park in Edmonton has more submarines than the armed forces. There is no evidence for the other choices.

**30.** (5)  Canada has only eighteen tanks. The passage tells you that Britain and West Germany have more tanks than that in their training centers in western Canada.

# ANSWER KEY

## CHAPTER 1: UNDERSTANDING WHAT YOU READ

### Exercise 1: Finding Details
### pages 19–20
Your wording may vary, but your answers should contain the same information as the answers below.
1. John Kennedy and Richard Nixon
2. Kennedy's good performance in the televised debates got him the extra votes he needed.
3. Seabrook, New Hampshire
4. May 1977
5. They would have to leave on one two-lane highway.
6. They want to prevent the completion and opening of the plant.

### Exercise 2: More Practice in Finding Details
### pages 20–22
1. (4) The first sentence tells you this.
2. (5) The second sentence tells you about a law against giving away food or drinks. The third sentence says Mr. Belair was arrested because of this law.
3. (2) The second sentence states that an American plane dropped the first atomic bomb.
4. (3) The third sentence states that the bomb destroyed the entire city.
5. (4) The second sentence states that competition from overseas has forced both sides to look at the way they work together. While the other statements could be true, only (4) is stated directly in the passage as the cause of cooperation.
6. (5) The fifth sentence states that the workers accepted pay cuts.

### Exercise 3: Synonym, Definition, and Comparison Clues
### pages 23–24
Your wording may vary, but your answers should contain the same information as the answers below.
1. a process of steel making consisting of blowing air through molten iron to get rid of impurities

2. phony cure-all
3. giving jobs and favors for political reasons
4. a company that controls production of a product and has no competition
5. amount of goods produced
6. crossing the continent, or coast to coast

### Exercise 4: Antonym and Contrast Clues
### page 25
1. (b) The contrast clue is "After years without restrictions on the number. . ."
2. (a) The clue is "contrasted sharply with the beauty."
3. (b) The arid West is contrasted with the well-watered East.
4. (b) The clue is "fighting broke out."
5. (c) The contrast is "unlike the Native American tribes, which only wanted to keep their own lands."

### Exercise 5: Using the Sense of the Passage
### pages 26–27
1. (3) The Wright brothers' flight in 1903 gives you a clue that it must be around 1900. In addition, the paragraph is talking about changes taking place over time, so the answer shouldn't be a specific year.
2. (3) The paragraph is full of examples of overcrowding—traffic jams, crowded elevators, and crowded subway trains.
3. (1) A tenement is a run-down slum building.
4. (3) Five decades of stemming tobacco would probably make hands twisted.

### Exercise 6: Recognizing Restated Information
### pages 28–29
1. I  They wanted "a chance to make money and go back . . ."
2. C  This sentence restates "The various teachers found a congenial atmosphere in our home . . ." *Congenial* means "friendly."

3. I  The passage states that Vanderbilt wanted political stability in the region, so he arranged the overthrow of an existing government. This type of action does not promote democracy.

4. C  This sentence restates information in the second paragraph. A coalition supported by Vanderbilt got rid of Walker after he quarreled with Vanderbilt.

## Exercise 7: Restating Information in Your Own Words
### pages 29–30

Your wording may vary, but your answers should contain the same information as the answers below.

1. Rockefeller forced the railroads to charge him low freight costs on his oil shipments.

2. Rockefeller would cut prices for his oil in areas where he had competitors.

3. The AFL promoted clear-cut issues such as rate of pay and the length of the workday.

4. They put up candidates for political office and asked for major changes in American society.

## Exercise 8: Summarizing Facts
### page 31

In this exercise, the correct summary is always the choice that contains all the important ideas from the three original statements.

1. (b)
2. (b)
3. (a)

## Exercise 9: Identifying Unrelated Sentences
### pages 33–34

1. (d)  The other sentences are all about the same topic, Tanya's new car.

2. (c)  The other sentences talk about American interest in Japanese products.

3. (c)  The topic of the other four sentences is the Consumer Price Index.

4. (e)  The topic of the other sentences is the textile industry.

## Exercise 10: Identifying the Main Idea
### pages 35–36

In this exercise, the main idea choice (M) is supported or explained by the details in the rest of the paragraph. The other choices are either too broad (B), too narrow (N), or not mentioned in the passage (X).

1. (a) B
   (b) N
   (c) X
   (d) M
2. (a) B
   (b) M
   (c) X
   (d) N
3. (a) M
   (b) N
   (c) X
   (d) B

## Exercise 11: Writing Topic Sentences
### pages 37–38

Although your wording will vary from the answers below, you should have written similar information. Compare your answers to these to be sure you were on the right track.

1. *Topic:* FDIC
   *Main Point:* FDIC protects people who deposit in a bank.
   *Topic Sentence:* The purpose of the Federal Deposit Insurance Corporation is to protect people against bank failure.

2. *Topic:* consumer co-ops
   *Main Point:* There are different kinds, but all are owned by members.
   *Topic Sentence:* Although there are different kinds of consumer co-ops, they are all owned by their members.

3. *Topic:* Shirley's financial problems
   *Main Point:* It's hard to make ends meet as a senior citizen.
   *Topic Sentence:* As a senior citizen, Shirley faced many financial problems.

## Exercise 12: Main Idea of a Passage
### pages 40–41

1. (a)  Choice (b) is not true. Choices (c) and (d) are details that tell you more about the main idea.

**2.** (c) Choices (a) and (d) are details. Choice (b) is not true.

**3.** (c) Choices (a) and (b) are details that tell you more about the main idea. Choice (d) is not true.

**4.** (b) Choice (c) is a detail mentioned only in paragraph 2, and choice (d) is a detail mentioned only in paragraph 1. Choice (a) is not true.

### Exercise 13: Chapter Review
### pages 42–44

**1.** (5) The passage is a story told by Harriet Hanson. She writes of what she thought and did during the beginning of a mill strike.

**2.** (2) The word *strike* is used in the third sentence of Harriet's story: "When the day came on which the girls were to turn out, . . . so many of them left that our mill was at once shut down." You can tell from this description that they were going on strike.

**3.** (4) There is a synonym clue: "irresolute, uncertain what to do. . . ."

**4.** (2) From what Harriet says, you can imagine that she might be pretending she wasn't afraid to strike. Harriet says she was impatient and childish, eliminating choices (1) and (4). Her following action and her pride in its result shows that she did have a sense of responsibility, eliminating choice (3). Her action was brave, eliminating choice (5).

**5.** (3) This is stated in the next to last sentence.

**6.** (3) This is stated in the fourth sentence.

**7.** (1) The main idea is stated in the first sentence. It is supported by two reasons: the poor commit more crimes, and the rich who commit crimes are able to stay out of jail.

**8.** (1) You must summarize the items listed in the second paragraph: knife, fork, cup, plate, drum, fife. These are all eating utensils and musical instruments.

**9.** (1) The final paragraph makes the topic clear: ". . . Our march had done its work. We had drawn the attention of the nation to the crime of child labor."

**10.** (5) This number is given in the first sentence.

## CHAPTER 2: CHARTS, GRAPHS, AND MAPS

### Exercise 1: Reading the Titles and Headings on a Chart
### page 48

The answers you wrote should be similar to these sample answers.

The **first** chart is about the ranking of the teams in the Atlantic Division of the NBA.

The **second** chart is about the budget figures for the BOCES Adult Learning Center.

### Exercise 2: Finding Information on a Chart
### pages 50–51

**1.** 39.2

**2.** Fish

**3.** Poultry

**4.** It decreased. The minus sign (−) tells you that consumption went down.

**5.** 0.4%

**6.** Coffee, tea, and cocoa. The word *decreased* tells you that you are looking for a minus sign (−). The largest percentage decrease was −21.1%.

### Exercise 3: Main Idea of a Chart
### pages 53–54

**1.** (2) In every occupation shown on the chart, women earn less than men. Choices (3) and (4) are true, but they are only details. Choices (1) and (5) are not based on the chart at all.

**2.** (1) The chart shows women earning a higher percentage of the degrees in each field except education. Choice (2) is true, but it is only a detail. Choices (3), (4), and (5) cannot be proven based on the chart.

### Exercise 4: Topic of a Graph
pages 55–56

The answers you wrote should be similar to the sample answers below.
**Graph 1** is about the changes in oil prices from 1970 to 1985.
**Graph 2** is about the percent of Indian people that belong to different religions.

### Exercise 5: The Main Idea of a Graph
pages 58–59

You wrote some of the answers to this exercise in your own words. The answers you wrote should be similar to the sample answers below.
1. This graph tells what it cost a hospital to take care of a patient for 7.6 days between 1978 and 1982.
2. The bars are getting taller, so costs are rising.
3. (2) This choice summarizes the information on the graph. Choices (1) and (3) may be true, but you can't be sure. Choices (4) and (5) are not based on the graph at all.
4. This graph gives a general idea of how people on welfare spend their money.
5. Food, rent, and utilities. These items are the largest parts of the graph.
6. (3) Food, rent, and utilities are necessities. Most of the graph is taken up by these items. Choice (1) is true, but it is only a detail. Choices (2), (4), and (5) are not based on the graph.

### Exercise 6: Reading Pictographs
page 61
1. **$200:** Each of the symbols stands for $100.
2. **Washington, D.C.:** It has the longest row of symbols.
3. **San Antonio:** It has only one symbol in its row.
4. **San Francisco's:** Comparing the rows for the two cities, you can see

that San Francisco has the shorter row.
5. (4) This choice pulls together all the information on the graph. Choice (2) is a detail. Choices (1), (3), and (5) cannot be proven by the graph.

### Exercise 7: Reading Bar Graphs
page 63
1. **Mexico:** The bar for Mexico is the only bar that stops between 60 and 65.
2. **55:** The bar for Peru stops at exactly 55.
3. **Sweden:** It has the tallest bar.
4. **Ethiopia:** It has the shortest bar.
5. **Four:** There are four bars shorter than the U.S. bar.
6. **About 35 years:** The bar for Ethiopia almost reaches 40. The bar for Sweden almost reaches 75; 75 − 40 = 35

### Exercise 8: Reading Line Graphs
pages 65–66
1. **1890:** The lowest point on the graph is at the year 1890.
2. **1970:** The highest point on the graph is at the year 1970.
3. **70%:** At 1960 on the horizontal scale, the data point is at 70% on the vertical scale.
4. (5) Each year, the graph shows a greater percentage of people living in urban areas.

### Exercise 9: Reading Circle Graphs
pages 67–68
1. **7.8%:** The label for the Education segment is at the top right corner. The percentage given with the label is 7.8%.
2. **Local aid:** This is the largest segment of the graph, 28.7%.
3. **Economic development:** Scanning the labels and percentages, you should pick out 4.3%. The label with that percentage is Economic development.
4. **Education:** The education segment is 7.8% of the total. The criminal justice and public safety segment is smaller, 5.2%.
5. **Over 70:** This is the smallest segment, only 1.5% of the total population.

6. **31–40:** This is the largest segment, 20.1% of the population.

7. **21–30:** Among the age groups under 60 years of age, 21–30 is the smallest segment, 8.5%.

8. **11–20:** Because these segments are almost the same size, you must read the percentages to answer correctly.

## Exercise 10: Direction and Distance on a Map
### page 71

1. **Thailand and Laos:** The arrow in the upper left corner of the map tells you north is up. Nations north of Cambodia must be above Cambodia on the map.

2. **South:** Takeo is directly below Phnom Penh on the map.

3. **Approximately 150 miles:** You must use the scale of miles to estimate this distance.

4. **The Gulf of Thailand:** It is below Battambang on the map.

5. **Approximately 125 miles:** You must use the scale of miles to estimate this distance.

## Exercise 11: Using a Map Key
### pages 73–74

1. **The Amazon River:** This is the only river shown on the map in the northern part of Brazil.

2. **Lake Mirini:** It is at the bottom of the map, in the southernmost portion of Brazil.

3. **Uruguay:** This country borders the southern tip of Brazil.

4. **Brasilia:** It is marked with the ⦿ symbol.

5. **The Equator:** The mouth of the Amazon is on the northern coast of Brazil at the Equator.

6. **Pico da Neblina:** Two high mountains are marked on the map with the + symbol. Pico da Neblina has the higher elevation.

## Exercise 12: Reading Historical Maps
### pages 75–76

1. (3) The Pawnee were in the region cutting through the center of the map. The key shows that the Plains Indians lived in this region.

2. (1) The farthest northern parts of the map match the Eskimo and Aleut section of the key.

3. (5) If you check the Southwest Indians portion of the map, you will find the Hopi Indians there.

## Exercise 13: Chapter Review
### pages 77–84

1. (5) Wyoming had 84 abortions per 1,000 live births. All the other rates listed on the chart are higher.

2. (2) If you look up New York on the chart, you will find that the rate given is 666.

3. (5) The rate for the entire U.S. is given at the top of the chart as 358. Compare this rate to the rates of choices (1)–(5). Tennessee has a rate of 324.

4. (1) The row of symbols for India is the longest row.

5. (2) The United States has the third longest row. You can double-check by comparing the figures listed under each row.

6. (5) The percentage of New Jersey residents living in cities of 100,000 or more dropped for each year shown on the graph. The other choices cannot be proven by the graph.

7. (3) The middle bar is for 1970. The percent for that bar is 15.5%.

8. (5) 1985 is the last year shown on the graph. At 1985 on the horizontal scale, the lines for *New York Daily News* and *USA Today* merge.

9. (4) The figures must be converted to millions on this graph. At the beginning of 1983, the line for the *Wall Street Journal* is at 2 on the vertical scale, which means 2,000,000 (2 million).

10. (4) This choice summarizes the data on the graph. The other choices cannot be proven by the graph.

11. (3) This percent is listed with the label for the car riders.

12. (2) If you scan the segments looking for 43.7%, you will find it with the school bus label.

13. (5) The area around San Francisco matches the key for more than 100 persons per square mile.

14. (1) Measure off 200 miles going straight up the map from San Diego. The area there matches the key for less than 25 persons per square mile.

15. (3) The key shows that South Carolina seceded first.

16. (2) Find the part of the key for slaveholding Union states. Then check each of the states that matches that part of the key. Only Kentucky is among the answer choices.

17. (4) Find Texas on the map. Then find the part of the key that matches Texas. That part of the key says "seceded Jan.– Feb. 1861."

18. (1) Find the regional boundary for West Tennessee. The only city shown in West Tennessee is Memphis.

19. (4) Find Nashville and look to the east. Knoxville is directly east of Nashville and is located on the Tennessee River.

20. (5) Find the western border of the state. It is labeled *Mississippi River*.

## CHAPTER 3: PATTERNS IN SOCIAL STUDIES READING

### Exercise 1: Putting Events in Sequence
pages 88–89
Passage 1

— Marshall discovers gold at Sutter's Mill.
— Marshall and Sutter test the stones to see if they are gold.
— Marshall sends gold seekers off to look for gold.
— Groups of men discover gold in the places where Marshall sent them.

Passage 2

Your timeline may not be exactly like this one. Are there at least three events on your timeline? Are the events in the correct time order?

earlier

— A cow kicked over a kerosene lamp.
— Fire spread through the West Side.
— The fire jumped the Chicago River.
— The fire was put out.
— Food, clothing, and money began pouring in.

later

### Exercise 2: Using Dates to Identify Sequence
pages 90–91

— Columbus discovers America.
— Cartier discovers the mouth of the St. Lawrence River.
— De Soto murders thousands of Indians at Mabila.
— Champlain establishes the fur trade with the Indians.
— Marquette and Joliet travel down the Mississippi River.

### Exercise 3: Sequence in Graphs
page 93

1. (1) Looking at the graph between 1965 and 1970 on the horizontal scale, you can see that the line goes up and then goes down.

2. (2) In 1975 NASA spending was between $3 and $4 billion. In 1980 it was almost $5 billion. By 1985 it was over $7 billion.

3. (5) This choice represents the pattern shown on the graph.

### Exercise 4: Expedition Maps
pages 95–96

1. (4) The box labeled *1* is De Soto's departure from Cuba. The box labeled *2* is his landing at Tampa Bay in present-day Florida.

2. (3) Trace De Soto's route and look for a box that tells you that friendly Indians supplied food. That box is labeled *7* and it is connected by a line to the dot labeled *Guaxulle*.

3. (4) Continue to trace De Soto's route, looking for his death. Box *13*, dated 21 May 1542, tells of De Soto's death.

4. (5) Scan the map to find the circle labeled *Quizquiz.* It is just below box *10,* which tells you that De Soto discovered the Mississippi River there.

### Exercise 5: Reading Maps of Historical Change
### page 97
1. T   The Oregon Country became part of the U.S. in 1846. Mexico ceded the Southwest in 1848.
2. T   The first major purchase shown on the map is the Louisiana Purchase in 1803. All the other new territories were added in later years.
3. F   The Gadsden Purchase (1853) followed the Mexican Cession.
4. F   Most of Florida was acquired in 1819.

### Exercise 6: Identifying Cause and Effect
### page 99
1. *What happened?* Colombia found itself in financial trouble. *Why did it happen?* The wholesale price of coffee had dropped 25%.
2. *What happened?* The American West developed rapidly after the Civil War. *Why did it happen?* Because of the railroads.
3. *What happened?* Oil prices increased dramatically. *Why did it happen?* The oil cartel OPEC was formed in 1973.
4. *What happened?* The price of natural rubber dropped. *Why did it happen?* Man-made rubber was developed.

### Exercise 7: Cause and Effect in a Passage
### pages 100–101
1. (3) The first sentence of the second paragraph says that the king of Portugal asked Vespucci to go after reading Vespucci's false story.
2. (1) The first sentence of the third paragraph tells you this. The clue word *because* makes the cause-and-effect relationship very clear.
3. (5) This is stated in the last sentence of the first paragraph.

4. (4) The second paragraph gives you this information. The clue *As a result* tells you that victims receiving less money is the result of lower damage awards in Indian courts.
5. (2) There is evidence for this answer throughout the passage: The children learned honesty through personal relationships. The children did what they saw others do. If the people the children imitated were honest, the children tended to be honest.

### Exercise 8: Applying Cause and Effect
### page 102
1. c   Laws banning discrimination against black voters led to a surge in the election of black officials.
2. d   Under the Civil Rights Act, blacks and whites had to be treated the same in public places such as buses.
3. b   Based on this decision, black and white children were segregated into different schools.
4. a   The Emancipation Proclamation issued by Lincoln encouraged slaves to come north to fight with the Union army.

### Exercise 9: Identifying Similarities
### page 104
The words you used in your answers may not be just like the words used in the sample answers below. However, you should have written the same information in your answers.
1. They stopped hunting and gathering food and started farming instead.
2. They are still hunters and gatherers.
3. They are large islands, located not far off the coast of a major continent.
4. They used to have great military strength and control huge empires.
5. They both have a lot of industries and do a lot of trading of goods.

**Exercise 10: Identifying Contrasts
page 106**

Uptown Jews were born in America and lived on New York's Upper East Side and Upper West Side; they did not keep kosher; and they were wealthy. Downtown Jews, on the other hand, were born in Eastern Europe and lived on the Lower East Side; they did keep kosher; and they were not wealthy.

**Exercise 11: Comparison and Contrast in Illustrations
pages 107–108**

1. T   To make sure this statement is true, you must check all the states to make sure none had an increase of less than 2%.
2. F   Tennessee had a higher percentage, 64%.
3. T   Although the lines for New York and Chicago are at different heights, both were going up during the same period—1880 to 1960.
4. F   New York has always been much larger than Chicago.
5. T   Both cities had just under 3 million people.
6. F   Chicago's population decreased between 1960 and 1980. Los Angeles gained population between 1960 and 1980.

**Exercise 12: Chapter Review
pages 109–112**

1. (2)   The area that matches the key for 1801 is all within these four states.
2. (2)   As the years passed, more cotton was grown in areas to the south and west (below and to the left) of the 1801 cotton-growing area.
3. (3)   The area that matches the key for 1839 shows the growth in cotton land between 1801 and 1839. Large portions of these four states are in this area.
4. (1)   The passage states, "Probably one of the main causes of the problem is peer pressure . . ." None of the other choices are given as possible causes by this writer.
5. (2)   The passage states, "The desperate need for money to buy drugs can lead the user to prostitution or robbery." These are crimes.
6. (1)   The first paragraph tells you that a high-tech boom gets started by new companies offering new products. The last sentence of the passage tells you that the pattern described in the passage applies to all three high-tech booms.
7. (4)   The last sentence of the passage lists the different products that created each boom.
8. (3)   The three paragraphs describe these steps in order. The first paragraph talks about a new product being created when thinkers don't have enough to do in a slow period. The second paragraph describes the industry boom that follows. The third paragraph describes the industry going into a slump.
9. (3)   The cause of the boom is stated in the first paragraph.
10. (2)   In the last paragraph, the writer states, "Then the public's love affair with the product ends. . . . Then the boom is over."

## CHAPTER 4: ANALYZING SOCIAL STUDIES PASSAGES

**Exercise 1: Fact or Opinion?
pages 114–115**

1. F
2. O
3. O
4. F
5. F
6. O
7. F

**Exercise 2: Facts and Opinions in a Passage
page 116**

**Passage 1**

a. O
b. F
c. F
d. F
e. O
f. O

**Passage 2**
   **a.** O
   **b.** F
   **c.** F
   **d.** F
   **e.** O
   **f.** O

## Exercise 3: Inferring Facts
## pages 118–119
**Part A**
Check to make sure you have the following information in your answers.
1. The speaker talks about seats, and the last sentence mentions a bus boycott.
2. The speaker says that the black community rallied to her support, so you can infer that she is black.

**Part B**
1. (2) The clues that Sam had an owner and was bought for $25 tell you that Sam was a slave.
2. (4) The speaker says, "Two hundred of us were working . . ." A factory would have that many workers. By using the pronoun *us*, she tells you she was one of the workers.
3. (5) You know the factory was multistory because there was a fire escape and stairs.
4. (3) The speaker says "When I took office . . . ," and he talks about proposing programs to Congress. You also can infer that he was president of the United States by eliminating the other choices.

## Exercise 4: Inferring Opinions
## pages 120–121
1. (1) The passage tells you how careful Roosevelt was to keep the public eye off his handicap. The last sentence of the passage says that this was a deliberate strategy. You can infer that Roosevelt was making sure that people thought he was healthy and able.
2. (4) The passage says that the Japanese used to be known for taking care of their elders. Now, in contrast, most Japanese don't feel they should have to support their parents.

3. (3) Elderly Japanese are having hard times because they are neglected by their families and forced to live alone on limited incomes. The Japanese need to find a way to take care of them.
4. (4) The speaker talks about "my daddy" and draws childlike pictures of "my house."
5. (5) The drawings show a "peace shield" stopping missiles from getting through to the house in the second frame. However, in the last frame, the house blows up in spite of the shield.

## Exercise 5: Analyzing Political Cartoons
## pages 124–126
You may have worded your answers differently from some of the sample answers below. Check to be sure you have the right information in your answer.
1.    Uncle Sam
2.    He is trying to reach around the whole world.
3. (2) Uncle Sam is clearly not succeeding in his efforts to reach around the world. Notice the desperate look on his face. He is trying to reach and hold on to too many places that are too far away.
4.    a bag of money
5.    money
6. (4) The cartoonist is saying that Boss Tweed controlled New York with money instead of intelligence.
7.    Mr. Taxes
8.    Recovery
9. (2) The cartoonist names the two fighters to show you what they stand for. Clearly, Mr. Taxes is beating up Recovery.

## Exercise 6: Distinguishing Fact from Hypothesis
## page 127
1. F
2. F
3. H
4. H

### Exercise 7: Finding the Author's Hypothesis
### pages 128–129

1. (3) In the last sentence, the author states that two- and three-bathroom houses are common because the extra bathrooms increase the resale value of a house.

2. (4) The author says that every college graduate who wants to get rich thinks that law is the way to do it.

3. (5) The passage states that members can have part of their paychecks deposited directly into their savings accounts and explains that this helps people build their savings.

### Exercise 8: Making a Reasonable Hypothesis
### pages 130–131

1. (3) Fisher heard about the ships by reading *The Treasure Hunter's Guide*. He put an extraordinary amount of time and money into his search. The evidence suggests that he was hoping it would pay off in valuable treasure.

2. (1) It makes sense that, if health insurance pays for most of the cost of medical care, people would be more likely to seek out care. There is no evidence for the other answers.

3. (4) In 1967, the doctors found that many people were hungry. The symptoms of the children were probably caused by their not getting enough to eat.

### Exercise 9: Identifying Probable Outcomes
### page 132

You should have checked the following.
1. c, d          2. b, c, d

### Exercise 10: Identifying the Author's Prediction
### pages 133–134

1. (3) The author says that many schools are appealing to older students in order to keep their enrollments up.

2. (2) In the third sentence, the author states that small farms are getting rarer.

3. (1) The author states that farms will get larger and larger and that small farms will continue to disappear.

4. (5) In the last sentence, the writer states that day-care centers in the workplace will become more common in the future.

### Exercise 11: Making a Prediction Based on a Passage
### pages 135–136

1. (4) It is clear from the passage that none of Bolivia's industries are really benefiting the country. Therefore, starting new industries would probably help Bolivia.

2. (1) If the price of tin rose, the tin mines could reopen. Then people would have jobs and more money would be coming into the country from the sale of tin.

3. (3) Because the Indians manage the plants themselves, there is reason for Choctaw youth to get an education. They have the opportunities to become managers and executives, not just unskilled workers.

### Exercise 12: Chapter Review
### pages 137–141

1. (3) The passage states, "He said nothing. Newspapers must have copy." You can infer that the newspapers started making things up about Coolidge because he gave them nothing else to write about.

2. (2) The passage implies that the real Calvin Coolidge did not reveal himself to the public. All the country had to go on was "his little witticisms, his dry wit"—not enough to get to know the real Coolidge.

3. (1) The tallest bar, 1 year and under, accounts for 55% of the people.

4. (3) Since the majority of people don't stay on welfare for more than a year or two, they must need the welfare payments only to get them through a rough period.

5.    He is talking to the reporters.

6. (4) The cartoonist shows the terrorist taking a hostage in front of a large group of reporters with cameras. The cartoon implies that getting attention from the press is the purpose of taking the hostage.

7. (2) The passage tells how different dance fads have come and gone. It is reasonable to expect that there will be another one soon.

8. (3) The only remaining Republican candidate has smears on his record, and Dukakis is already a popular governor. It is reasonable to expect that he will be re-elected.

9. (5) In the second paragraph, the author says "Prices may be going up because people expect them to go up." In addition, he says that people are willing to pay a high price for a house if they think the price will continue to rise.

10. (1) In the last paragraph, the author describes how prices leveled off in California and says that the same thing will happen in Tristan.

11. (1) In the last two sentences, the authors state that education was the key to success.

## CHAPTER 5: EVALUATING SOCIAL STUDIES MATERIALS

### Exercise 1: Is There Enough Information?
pages 143–144
1. ✓
2. X
3. X
4. ✓
5. X
6. ✓
7. ✓
8. X

### Exercise 2: Using Information on a Map
page 145
1. ✓
2. X
3. X

4. ✓
5. ✓
6. X

### Exercise 3: Identifying Irrelevant Information
page 147
You may have worded your answer differently from the sample answers below. Check to be sure you included the correct information in your answers.

**Passage 1**
a. The writer wants people to vote for Gil Cohen for mayor.
b. The irrelevant reasons are (1) he is more attractive than his opponent and (2) he has spent over $100,000 of his own money to get elected.

**Passage 2**
a. The writer wants to convince someone that the contract for building the K9 missile should be given to General Progress.
b. The irrelevant reasons are (1) its home office is in the writer's district and (2) General Progress has contributed to his reelection campaign.

### Exercise 4: Using Information Correctly
pages 148–149
1. (3) The last sentence tells you that this event raised millions of dollars to feed hungry Americans.

2. (5) The passage gives examples of Americans raising money for charitable causes.

3. (4) The third sentence of the passage tells you that affirmative action programs try to correct past prejudice. The passage does not contain enough information to prove any of the other choices.

4. (3) The second sentence tells you that, in a kibbutz, most things are owned by everyone as a group. The other choices are not mentioned in the passage.

5. (1) The passage tells you that people over thirty-five are usually set in their ways and unable to adjust to the needs of the kibbutz. There is no evidence for the other choices.

## Exercise 5: Recognizing Errors in Reasoning
### pages 150–151
1. a. X
   b. ✓
2. a. ✓
   b. X
3. a. X
   b. ✓

## Exercise 6: Errors in Reasoning
### pages 152–153
You may have worded your answers differently from the sample answers below. Check your answers to be sure they contain the correct information.
1. (2)  The writer says he was doing much worse than he had been four years before, so he voted for Reagan.
2.      The problem is that the reasons he was doing badly (his wife dying, his children dropping out of school, his drinking and losing his job) had nothing to do with the president or the government. These factors should not have influenced his vote.
3. (2)  The passage tells you that the unhappiest group was married women.
4.      The problem is that she thinks the results of the study are wrong based on the experience of only one person: herself.
5. (3)  The writer's reasoning is correct. The role of the FBI as a government agency is to protect citizens from crime.

## Exercise 7: Recognizing Values
### pages 155–157
1. (2)  The passage says many people buy the coins because they are pure gold. Gold is valuable and a good investment.
2. (3)  The passage says that the people who oppose the sale of Krugerrands are hoping to pressure the South African government into treating blacks and whites equally.
3. (3)  The caption of the cartoon tells you that Reagan would like to be free from the press, which would mean he would not be criticized by reporters and newswriters. This would add greatly to his power.
4. (1)  The cartoonist makes Reagan and his advisors look sinister as they talk about not liking the press. Since the cartoonist is part of the press, it is likely that he would value freedom of the press.
5. (2)  The purpose of buying the old farm would be to save the land for education and recreation.
6. (5)  The arguments against buying the old farm were related to its cost. Although the voters were in favor of preserving open land, they were more concerned about the cost of the project.

## Exercise 8: Propaganda and Advertising
### pages 159–161
1. (5)  The ad says that Budweiser is America's highest-quality beer, using only the finest barley and hops. It implies that other beers are made from lower-quality ingredients.
2.      Answers will vary.
3. (3)  The ad implies that a Ferrari is for a daring, or adventurous, person.
4. (1)  The ad implies that you will look like the muscle-man in the "After" picture if you use this program. Men who want to look like a muscle-man would be attracted to the ad.
5. (4)  The ad implies that, if you shop at Leslie's, you will look sophisticated.

## Exercise 9: Political Propaganda
### pages 162–163
1.      They had slowed down six Soviet armies, and they had been "purified" by the defeat.
2. (4)  Goebbels didn't want the Germans to think they were losing the war. If the real extent of the disaster were known, people might become angry with the German government and military leaders.

**3.** (2)  The ad says, "Now is the time to join the Hart bandwagon," or join the other supporters of Hart. None of the other choices are mentioned in the ad.

**4.** (4)  The poster talks about Mussolini loving children and children loving him, and he is pictured with a small child. None of the other choices are implied.

### Exercise 10: Chapter Review
### pages 164–168

**1.** (3)  The caption reads, "The Sauce for Kings." None of the other choices are mentioned in the ad.

**2.** (5)  There is no dark line from Jacksonville to Savannah, so there was no railroad.

**3.** (4)  All the train lines end just beyond the Mississippi. Anyone wanting to go farther west would have to travel another way.

**4.** (2)  The passage says that Amnesty International watches out for human rights throughout the world.

**5.** (3)  Since the purpose of the organization is to promote human rights, you would want to know if it was accomplishing that purpose. The other choices would not tell you whether it was accomplishing that purpose.

**6.** (4)  The passage describes all the violent conflicts that rage in the world in spite of the efforts of the United Nations to keep the peace. The passage does not support the other choices.

**7.** (5)  The first sentence tells you that the United Nations was founded to help nations solve their differences peacefully.

**8.** (3)  In the lower left-hand corner, a question asks, "What's a nice girl like you doing in a place like this?" The question implies that Liberty should not be at this celebration. Having Liberty dressed in a wet T-shirt shows the tasteless, commercial nature of the celebration. In addition, Liberty's T-shirt reads "hype." The cartoonist is saying that the celebration was meaningless hype.

**9.** (4)  The ad does not tell you much about Mr. Amorelli's ideas. You would want to find out more before you decided whom to vote for.

**10.** (3)  Experience usually partly determines what a person's work is worth. The other choices do not relate to what a person's work is worth.

**11.** (1)  Only this choice relates to the quality of the glove.

## CHAPTER 6: APPLYING INFORMATION IN SOCIAL STUDIES

### Exercise 1: Applying Information in Everyday Life
### pages 171–172

**1.** (5)  The passage states that exercising for at least fifteen minutes at least three times a week is the most effective way to lose weight.

**2.** (4)  The passage says that the greatest office need will be people trained to use modern equipment (such as computers).

### Exercise 2: Applying Information in a Passage
### pages 173–174

**1.** H
**2.** A
**3.** R
**4.** H
**5.** no
**6.** yes
**7.** yes
**8.** no

### Exercise 3: Applying Map Skills
### pages 175–176

**1.** Take Route 5 south to Route 84 east to Route 80 east.

**2.** Take Route 8 east to Route 10 east.

**3.** (4)  The airport is on the Blue Line.

North Station in on the Orange Line. The two lines intersect at State.

4. (3)  Harvard is on the Red Line. Science is on the Green Line. The two lines intersect at Park St.

### Exercise 4: Applying Information on Charts and Graphs
### pages 178–179

1. (3)  According to the graph, in 1970 there were more than 4 million working women. In 1984, there were about 8 million working women.

2. (3)  The graph shows many women with children under six in the work force. Day care at their workplace is likely to appeal to these women.

3. **Blackdeck Desktop:**  This phone is the easiest to use of all the phones described. A man with arthritis in his hands would need a phone that is easy to use.

4. **Sunbrand Slimphone:**  This phone is the most durable of all the phones, so it would be most likely to hold up under heavy use.

5. **Homephone Basic:**  This is the least expensive phone of the four.

### Exercise 5: Chapter Review
### pages 180–183

1. (5)  First find Rochester and Corning on the map. Then find the route that is closest to a straight line.

2. (2)  First find Syracuse and Bath on the map. Then find the route that is closest to a straight line.

3. (3)  The Dodge Rainbow has the highest highway gas mileage and the best repair record of the choices given.

4. (2)  The Chevrolet Pony has a better repair record than the Ford Flicker, which is the only other car listed that is in Libby's price range.

5. (4)  The passage says that fields are preserved in case they are needed for food production in the future. Tobacco is not a food.

6. (3)  In the last paragraph, the author says that teens have nothing useful or important to do. Therefore, their energy comes out in destructive acts.

7. (5)  Community service work would give teens a positive outlet for their energy. Therefore, they would not need to commit crimes to use up their energy.